MY VIBE

JEREMY SIGLER

MY VIBE

SPOONBILL BOOKS

I

Presumably

since it happened close to thirty years ago, word has gotten out by now to the general public that I nearly died the same way the lead singer of the Yardbirds died.

I was in Felton's basement where we usually practiced. We were, I'm proud to say, pre-grunge, and post-Joy Division. Anyway, the phone rang, and when Paul ran to get it, he handed me his bass instead of setting it down.

I was holding my guitar with one hand and when I went to take Paul's, I was seized by a strong electrical current. The current encircled my fingers and hands and began to climb up my arms towards my heart. I was now locked to both guitars, totally paralyzed, with my body being elevated off the ground. All I could think was: fuck.

Then, somehow, I was discharged—thrown clear across the room, where, miraculously, I landed gently on my back. I cleared a sofa, and just missed a wood-burning stove.

I stood up in a daze, and looked over at my bandmates, who were standing in awe. Muth was looking at me like a laughing hyena too shocked to laugh. Felton looked like a toddler at a magic show. I was utterly humbled as I walked back across the room and viewed both guitars, which were now crisscrossed on the floor vibrating. One of the bass strings was even glowing. It was incandescent. Like a coil in a toaster oven. And there was a flame coming off it!

Weinstock, our drummer, shook his head as he fished out a smoke.

Tugged by the

gravity of Mott Street, I followed myself. South-east. I hustled out of my clothes and deposited myself facedown on the table.

The Chinese lady got started. After a few minutes she inquired about my poetry. My face remained buried in the padded donut.

Then she began to say something about me being a great writer. And her daughter this. And her daughter that. I lifted my head and turned around. Blood rushing back into my sinuses. "Was I willing to do what?"

The Chinese lady then slowly repeated that she wanted to trade five hours of massage for five hours of tutoring. Her fourteen-year-old daughter desperately had to improve her English scores in order to test into Hunter's gifted and talented program.

Monday afternoon, my phone rang. It was the Chinese massage lady! She asked if I was still planning to come and tutor her daughter. I'd forgotten all about it! But I still had time to get there. I quickly shut down my computer, and hustled out the door of my office.

I fought my way up a densely packed Mott Street, and swung open the door to the spa. I hadn't ever seen the place in the daytime. Nor through sober eyes. There was so much detail: a tourist sitting in one of the padded reclining La-Z-Boys having her feet rubbed. And in the seat next to her, a chubby little Chinese girl with a mouth full of braces, doing her best to clean a buffalo wing. Her lips were smeared with hot sauce. The entire place smelt like chicken wings.

The Chinese massage lady spotted me instantly and came right over. She seemed to be extremely appreciative. She gently took my arm, and in a frightening command of terse syllables, ordered her daughter to follow.

We turned the corner and she slid open the cheap door to the same closet-size massage room we always used. To my surprise, the room had been converted into a kind of make-shift classroom. The massage table now served as a desk, flanked by two metal folding chairs. A cozy lamp had been placed on the desk, along with a generous stack of lined paper. And three sharpened pencils.

I like

the idea of a poetry shop. It would be a kind of urban or suburban or even rural happening where one "shops" around for words, syllables, letters, or just punctuation. Say, a two-foot comma.

9

Often a camera is used. Walker Evans used a camera in 1930 to create that giant poetry shop, DAMAGED. He took a picture of the big-lettered marquis sign. As it was being carefully lowered off the back of a flatbed truck. Or was it being raised onto the flatbed? Either way, it was a very successful shop.

At times, the letter—like, say, the giant asparagus-piss-colored letter *M* of the word *McDonald's*—simply has to be shopped. The word has to be dismantled. In the middle of the night. Hauled off. And warehoused. Or brought home. To join the family of other letters. Cleverly, a word like *_cDonald's* becomes manifest the next morning. Alone on its big shaft in the sky.

Commanding roadside letters often make really good lawn art. Or endtables. A single letter can be the size of a chair.

The beautifully shopped word *Televis_on* is currently being stored in the weedy backyard behind my neighborhood bar, Henry Public. All the letters are there but one. The sign seems to have come from the television repair shop that was previously at that location.

My

shrink advised I get a dog. An Emotional Support Dog. He went so far as to write me an official letter granting me permission to bring this ESD with me on planes and trains. And buses.

I haven't gotten the dog yet. But just having a letter from my doctor folded in my wallet puts me at ease. When I do get the dog, I know what I'll name it: Placebo.

Thank God. Emotional support is on the way. Is this anything like a "supporter," also known as a jockstrap? Maybe I wouldn't need so much support if I were to let my life just hang.

Or drop. Like when a big walnut drops off a branch and lands with a thud in a shady patch of grass near the sandbox.

What if I drop out? I could get one of those campers. The kind that configures to the bed of a pickup. Like the one that family lives in during their month on Montague Street every year. When they come to sell trees the day after Thanksgiving.

Or I could get a big industrial crane to lift my mom's old Volkswagen camper up above the ginkgoes and set it down softly on the roof of my brownstone. And that's where I'll live. In the Vanagon. A city poet. With a kind of modest homebase.

I'll be like the poet illustrated in the Carl Spitzweg painting from 1839. He sits in bed under a blanket with his knees up. Deep in his writing. And he keeps an open umbrella in bed with him. Presumably this was his solution for the leaky ceiling directly over his bed. He heats the room by burning his early drafts.

I was on

one of my weeklong procrastination binges. All I could do was compulsively check and re-check my inbox. And YouTube the Beach Boys. Anything for a little relief.

I had to find some way to be productive. So I asked my intern—the one who recently called me a "douche"—to assist in a difficult task. "There's one girl left," I explained. "One girl from my past, who I've yet to stalk."

"Stalk?"

"Yeah. I guess that would be the word for it. Her name is Becky. And something keeps telling me that today is the day. That she's matured enough to regret certain, um, missed opportunities." I wondered, had I refrained from stalking her in order to give her time to reach this critical fork in the road? Did I really believe that she'd achieved a state of Chekhovian ennui?

All I knew for sure was that I was ready to stalk. So I instructed my intern to type the name Becky Bower into Google. I stood over her shoulder watching with anticipation. Nothing. Not a thing. So I told her to keep at it—to try all the possible variations of her name (i.e. Rebecca). My intern spent the rest of the morning working on it, sadly with no results.

Eventually, sometime after lunch, her computer must have felt sorry for us, or appreciated our persistence, or something, for it coughed up an image. An absolutely stunning family portrait of Becky and her four beautiful daughters…and her preppie, more or less pink, husband. They were at some steeplechase in Maryland. According to the picture's small caption, Becky was the owner and trainer of one of the thoroughbreds running in that day's race.

Within a few minutes, my clever intern, who was beginning to get into the spirit of things, had managed to obtain an email address. She opened up a blank document, and nodded for me to begin.

What came out of my heart felt like a flair shot from a life raft.

About three weeks later, long after I'd given up hope of ever hearing back from her, in came the most outstanding reply. It was virtually packed with triple exclamation points. There should be a word for such a thing: !!!. "Of course I remember you!!!" Becky wrote. "Do you remember me??? What do you remember???"

I promptly began to dictate a response: I remember kneeling at my locker to get my books. Your locker was right above mine. You'd often come in and get your books just as I was getting mine. You'd go up on your toes, which left me pretty much at eye-level with your flexed calves. It was this same routine every day.

I'd set my hand on your calf. And glide it up your leg. Inch by inch. Under the back of your skirt, going right up to the edge of your butt, but stopping at the elastic line of your panties. Then, after a pause, I'd keep going on top of your panties (never under), up onto your wonderful ass. And I'd give this ass a soft pinch. You'd look down at me, smile, and politely ask me to stop.

What else do I remember? Let me see...I remember being in Mr. Smoot's biology class dissecting my formaldehyde-soaked lab rat. You were across the room at another table dissecting your rat. Something compelled me to take my scalpel, cut out my rat's long intestine, sneak up behind you, and lace it over your shoulders and around your neck.

I remember the night I drove in past the guard station up onto McDonogh's sleepy winter campus. The leafless trees were limber like deft fingers on a trumpet. You had gotten permission to meet with a visitor. It was a school night, I remember, and we both had homework.

13

We were alone for the first time. In a windowless basement with lemony cinderblock walls. We sat for some time on the durable blocky furniture, and then, somehow—I have no idea how—we became entwined in a real kiss. I must have been copying something I'd seen in a movie when I swept my hand across the top of the table, sending a bunch of things flying: a heavy book bag, a Sony Walkman, my wrinkled navy blazer. You were now pinned under me, and I was uncoupling your bra with two fingers, while simultaneously jamming my other hand down the front of your panties. I was on your neck too. Just like Jack! Like Jack? Um…That's it! Jack!!! That's who I was being. Jack Nicholson. I was kind of doing to Becky what Jack does to Jessica Lange in the bakery in *The Postman Always Rings Twice*.

And now, almost thirty years later, here I am, at work, standing behind my intern (who at least has a great sense of humor), watching her use my company card to reserve me a seat on the next southbound Amtrak out of Penn Station.

So that I can step onto the grounds of Becky's stable, walk past the snorting horses, like any Native American poet worth his salt, and get reacquainted with my old friend. Then, we'll continue our long-paused kiss. And our rape scene.

And after our rape scene, I'll ride off with Becky, clung to her back, holding on for dear life. And I'll whisper in her ear: Please train me. Train me just as you train your horses. Train me to be a champion. Train me to know that I am the voice of my generation.

often charge through. Stampede in a way. And I just try to keep my hat on and type through the storm.

I try to stay on point. While each point expands into its own universe and comes to rest inevitably off point.

I knew you were coming today. And I read a few poems. And found them to be kind of self-conscious. Because they sounded like they were trying too hard, or like I was attempting to chart something. To chart names. And places. They're, um, caught up, I think.

I want to change pace. When I would go to see Lilly, I'd lay down like this. And she'd sit behind me. And I'd just start. And it would always take me some place ripe. I'd sense her. She'd be suspended right over me. Hanging like a branch heavy with watery fruit. And there I'd be out on the plank—what I came to think of as Plankticus Erectus.

Even now, as I try to talk to you, I'm, I'm, trying to smarten my sentences. Fuck smart! I want to return to something more inchoate. Even if, in order to accomplish this, we are forced to stretch this dictation session out over the course of a whole afternoon, until I'm like producing gibberish.

This is why I just decided to cancel with Eileen. To cancel anything social. And I hope you too have nowhere to be.

Today I can feel Lake Tahoe calling. Crisp mountain air fanning the sun. The windows are all the way open. I can hear truck horns and cars lightly brushing the snare. And choppers. Idling trucks. I can hear the horse hooves clacking. Wouldn't it be nice? Can you say that line back to me in falsetto?

I was just sitting out on the stoop waiting for you. There was a steady stream of motivated people walking and working. Everywhere everyone. One guy was painting a door. Another was doing masonry on the steps of a brownstone. There were like three or four contractors in trucks pulled over to the edge of the sidewalk eating sandwiches.

The setting looked like a children's book by Richard Scarry. The one with pigs and bunny rabbits playing fireman and electrician. *What Do People Do All Day?* That's the title. Isn't that a hilarious title? What do I do all day? What uniform do I wear?

I guess this is my uniform. I guess this is my job. What we're doing right now. I guess this is what I do all day. Lay on my back with my heavy head hanging off the edge and you right there behind me typing away furiously. Keeping up with me and resting with my every pause.

I feel like a wire hanger. The air gets hung on me like a shirt. My production is to just be here for the air. To harness the air.

Let's

meet for lunch. In SoHo. We'll pretend it's the 80s. Back when the Apple Store was a sad old sack of bulk mail. Back when a grouchy man with a herniated disk sat behind a bulletproof window licking stamps. I would have to go there all the time, and stand in line, and wait to face the grouch.

Annina's gallery was directly across the street. Prince Street to be exact. Ahhh. Ahhh-neee-naaa. The ballroom dancer. The Basquiat dealer. A nasty rumor, still with her. Of torture. But to know Annina, is actually to know her Lucille Ball-ish ways.

One day she was trying to make a big sale to a very rich collector, when she started playing one of her games. Always, when the pressure was on, a game.

She called me into her office and commanded me to attach this, like, thirty-foot garden hose to the faucet in her bathroom, and to unfurl it over her desk, across the room, and right over the lap of the well-dressed Venezuelan gentleman seated on the couch with his legs crossed elegantly. He was trying to decide whether to buy the last remaining sizable Basquiat canvas in Annina's personal collection.

Annina got up and came over to the window with me. She helped me up onto the ledge, and braced me as I made one pretty hazardous step out onto the fire escape. She then made an overly dramatic effort to feed the hose up to me, as if we were two firefighters arriving at a raging second story blaze.

I climbed up one story with the nozzle in my hand, pulling the hose behind me. Once I was in perfect position over the glass roof, I yelled down to Annina giving her the signal to tango back into the bathroom in her flats, and crank on the water.

Water immediately began to cascade from my hose, and I directed the geyser at the sole persistent leaf. My objective.

Annina and the amused collector stood under the sunroof looking up at me, my leaf, and the water cascading from my hose. They were both smiling. Perhaps they were even making fun of me. I sprayed and sprayed and sprayed, trying

17

to get the little stubborn leaf to give up. Finally after about five minutes, the little stubborn leaf lost its strength and let go. And slid down to the gutter.

At pretty

much every party someone asks me to tell the story of my A.P.C.'s. I wear my A.P.C. jeans every day for about two years. They are my only pants. They never get washed. Washing them is forbidden. I'm not sure where this rule is officially stated, but I certainly live by it. And after about two years, when they've been tamed, broken in—by the time my boxers are visible through the void in my frayed crotch—I know it is time to bring them in.

I enter through the door of the SoHo boutique, where I am generally greeted by an attractive shopkeeper, who looks me up and down and nods approvingly. She then goes to a shelf at the back of the store and quickly returns with a brand new pair, in just my size. She hands over the stiff, navy square of denim. I force my legs into them, turn up the cuffs, and squat five times, feeling that memorable seizure of my crotch.

As I enter the new pair, the old pair, my soft gems, are laid across the oak countertop, and examined. As if by a palm reader. Every crease and crinkle is deeply admired. She then pops off the top of a Sharpie and hands it to me. By now I know the drill. I sign my initials discreetly on the inside of the waist band, just above the black and silver A.P.C. tag. At this point my jeans are swept off to the back of the boutique and hung on a special rack. I will never see them again. They will sit on this rack, getting wheeled out from time to time for A.P.C. VIPs.

Even with a frayed hole where my testicles once fought a war for ball room (and won, thank you!), the jeans can fetch up to three grand.

I know what you're thinking. And the answer is N-O. Positively not. Why wouldn't I go ahead and sell them on eBay and take the three grand? Good question. I guess I really must enjoy the glamour of walking into A.P.C. and initializing them as though they were a work of art. I must really enjoy this rare moment of acknowledgment.

So there I was, at Eva's apartment, dragging out my story, throwing back one of the last Red Stripes in the fridge, when I noticed that it was past 2:00 am. My audience had dwindled down to me and maybe two or three other alcoholics. This is when I was hit with a truly sensational idea: "Eva," I announced boldly, "I'd like to present you with a very special birthday present!" I'd already begun to unbuckle my belt and rip apart my button fly. "I want you to have these," I said, letting my perfect A.P.C.'s drop to my ankles, and stepping out of them into just my boxers. "I want them to be hung right here on this wall. OK?"

And before Eva had time to respond, I found some pushpins, climbed up on a chair and hung the jeans above the fireplace mantle. Horizontally! Then I stepped back to observe my work.

There they were. A stranger to me now. With my old leather belt still in the loops. And with my leather wallet still protruding from my back pocket. And, Jesus, even my iPhone.

About an hour later, I arrived by foot in front of my stoop. I was in only my boxers, a T-shirt, and sneakers. I went to dig at the usual spot for my keys. Only then did I realize I had no pockets.

I miss

the O.J. trial. I still check up on it from time to time. I've come to believe that O.J.'s son Jason was the killer. I can just feel it. I'm Hamlet.

But when I acted in a high school production of *Hamlet,* I didn't get the lead. On the contrary, I was assigned the tiny part of the English Ambassador. I basically had one line. And I only appeared on stage like two minutes from the end of the, like, four-hour play. "Rosencrantz and Guildenstern are dead." That was my line.

I'd usually cut it pretty close, arriving at school near the end of the second act. I'd enter back stage only a few minutes before going on. If I'd been drinking—which was pretty much always the case—I'd just go out on stage somewhat tipsy and say my damn line. Then there'd be the obligatory curtain call. Yeah right. Take a bow for my one friggin' line?

I'd split right away. Hop in my Isuzu Trooper II and shift gears back to my place around the keg out in the abandoned dirt patch of a semi-built suburb. The day of the matinee, I was so out of it that I forgot to get in costume. And I flubbed my damn line. "Guildencrantz and Rosenstern are dead,"

I said. In the same pair of huge gray sweatpants I slept in the night before.

I forward

songs. They are basically love letters. When I think Eva, I link Eva. Beware, some songs can get clogged and loop in the mind repeatedly. All day long. Which may not be appreciated by Eva or any other target of seduction. Links like this should come with a warning label.

Jonathan Schwartz—one of the weekend deejays on public radio—is a real problem. If you are ever listening to NPR on a Saturday morning and you experience an extended silence, please know that I am responsible for this sudden peace. Please know that I am the one who went downtown, broke into the radio station, broke into the studio, gagged Jonathan Schwartz, froze him like a mummy in silver duct tape, and left—leaving him there on the carpeted studio floor gagged and bound.

But at present, Schwartz is going strong. With his lounge act versions of Joni Mitchell songs, and tone-deaf Sinatra recordings.

And no matter what we do, we can't turn it off. Or change the station. Because our Bose-thingy doesn't have any buttons on it. It came with just a remote control. But the remote control has been lost for like three years.

And you know what else? The crappy Bose-thingy never ejected my favorite Arto Lindsay disc.

I've been having a hard

time breathing lately. And I mentioned this to my friend, who told me of an acupuncturist who once punctured her patient's lung. By accident, of course. Ugh.

Now I'm paranoid that my neighbor punctured my lung! I interrogated her about it while we were in the park last weekend. "Did you puncture my lung?" I asked. And she explained that such horrific things have been known to happen. But she assured me that in our therapy, she had not yet stuck any needle anywhere near my lungs. She'd only worked on my knee caps.

When she stood up, she was backlit by the sun. I squinted at her from my spot in the grass. I could see the perfect silhouette of her legs and the outline of her pussy hair through the sheer fabric of her dress. And that's not all. There was also a short little string directly between her thighs. I guess it was the string of her tampon or something. Hard to believe the sun could have produced so much information. So much evidence. So much drama.

I've since questioned numerous women about this sort of exhibitionism. They've all agreed that a woman knows the visibility of her pussy at all times relative to a man's roving eye. And so, "the show" had to have been intentional. My acupuncturist had to have been well aware that she was a walking shadow puppet theater putting on a play just for me.

Did you know

that the Genius Bar at the Apple Store is meant as a joke? Who are they making fun of? Themselves? I mean…I really believe in the concept of a genius. Don't they? You better believe they do.

Let me get into this. They're not your average technological grease monkeys, as the auto mechanics used to be called. They really are smart bartenders, in the sense that they're motivated by something…something cyber, I guess. And they make me feel a whole lot better about my device. And my human desire, in general.

But why must they resort to this jaded insincere IRONIC use of the word *genius?* Maybe this is Apple's way of helping their army get over themselves. Aimed at the symptom of a deeper psychological growing pain. Genius, here, means: we are comfortable using the word *genius* because we are all grown up now.

I can tell you one thing, I don't care if my bartender thinks of himself as a genius or not when he's refilling my pint. Nor do I care if my Apple Genius bartender thinks of himself as a genius. And while we all know that it may not take a genius to diagnose a laptop, it does indeed take a highly skilled person with amazing communication skills, who can remain poised, while the rest of us are in a total panic.

In the frightening fog of one of these panics—long before the days of Genius Bars and Apple Stores—I once had no choice but to send my computer to some tech support plant somewhere. First they sent me a special padded box with step-by-step instructions. I said goodbye to my laptop and placed it in the foam-lined box, and in a few days I received a call informing me that it had arrived at its destination in, like, Cincinnati. "I'm happy to report to you that there's absolutely nothing wrong with your hard drive," they said. "Your computer started right up. Like normal."

"Nothing's wrong?" I moaned. "But when I pushed in the on-off button, the machine didn't respond. The screen was jet black. And I know you know how horrifying that is. And the start up jingle? No jingle. Not a sound!"

"In the future," said the genius, "here's what you do: press in the *on* button, and KEEP it in. For, like, two seconds. Count, *one Mississippi, two Mississippi.*"

So that's what genius boils down to! But really. Genius is no joke. And to you sarcastic little fuckers, I want you to know I'm on to you. I say, back the fuck off! Do you hear the Clint in my voice?

I had an undergrad one semester who presented a framed Mensa certificate as his thesis project. There on the wall, all by itself, was this simple diploma. It was signed and stamped. And it had some kind of gold seal. We were all standing at a distance as he explained that it had just come in the mail, weeks after his on-line exam. He'd barely had time to get it framed. I walked up to the wall and stood before the work of art.

So I somehow managed

to get addicted to heroin. But the funny thing is that I didn't even know it was heroin. Until, like, yesterday. I'm now up to

24

three pills. But there are only, like, six pills left. And I'm happy for that plastic container that says "take one every four hours," because at least I know that I am only tripling it, which couldn't be close to an overdose. I guess. It just doesn't seem like Heath could have died from only three. No way. But he was also on other stuff. And, well, um, I am too. Like my asthma inhaler. And my nasal inhaler! Ha ha. That's a funny confession.

When I was down in Florida visiting my parents, I remember going into the bedroom and clawing through this little purse I was traveling with and popping one, like, every time someone raised their voice. Ah relief. Usually it would have turned into an O'Neill play in our kitchen—a feeding frenzy on dangling bits of anxiety. I was like, "It don't worry me." Like the girl at the end of *Nashville* who finally gets her chance with the mic, right after the real singer is assassinated and like bleeding through her white gown all over the guy in the Nudie Suit who is, like, running her to an ambulance screaming for help. I friggin' love the fuck out of *Nashville*. How else can I say it? I'm…ahhhhhhh. Let me catch my breath.

Sorry, no words can express it.

So, I was using the stuff after the wisdom tooth extraction, and I realized it was even better on an empty stomach. With a drink. I found that one pill followed by one hundred laps at the Y and a glass of Pinot Grigio was just right. At that round table at Brooklyn Social, way out on Smith Street near Carroll. Gums numb. My cell phone like *spin the bottle* on the table at the tip of my fingers waiting for a return text.

I called my dad yesterday and told him that with my lower back the Tramadol is effective but makes me a bit edgy, and that I'd much prefer the other pills. And he warned me, "Those are a controlled substance and they are highly addictive." Yeah yeah. I was, like, "I know."

But really, I didn't want to reveal my desperation. Or to expose the truth that I was trying to trick him into writing me a lifetime Life is Good prescription. Should I go back to the lower back guy, Dr. Chen, and pretend to be in agony? I remember that cryptic pain chart in his examination room with five faces. I had to point to the one I most resembled: the smiley face? The frowning face? The frowning crying face? The sobbing face! Ugh. I'm hooked.

But really, I am just trying to figure out if I can keep up this daily habit with a dwindling supply. By the way, I took a new Life is Good cap from my dad's stash (he has like ten of them) when I was down in Naples. So now I have that stick figure golf guy on my head. Just like the picture I saw of Robert Frank in the Steidl catalogue that just came.

He is me. Even though I've never even swung a golf club. I just know it, my poem—this poem!—is my hole-in-one. Watch it glide across that green and drop in the cup. Watch it glide! Watch it drop! In the cup!

And the two pills yesterday, while I was teaching in the snowstorm, pretty much made me feel like I was more than okay. In the groove. And that's golf. And teaching. I remember pulling open the blinds in the classroom and saying, "Watch my movie! Watch my movie!" I was referring simply to the snow scene out the window, which looked just like the famous whiteout in *McCabe and Mrs. Miller*. We've lucked out, Bob and I. We get these cinematic moments just when they're needed.

And then school got cancelled and Julian offered to drive me back to Brooklyn. And I slammed back a third pill in the men's room in the remainder of my cold coffee. We stopped for a glass of wine in a bar on Atlantic Ave. I vaguely remember the bartender topping me off a few times. I told Julian about my McKitchen concept (an actual industrial McDonald's kitchen, fully stocked, installed in your McMansion). And, of course, I told Julian all about my Lacanian analyst. I told him how after six years of psychoanalysis, it was ultimately that one glimpse she gave me of her panties that cured me. Transference. Countertransference. Then my language got dirty, and dirtier. A few visits later, and I was like no longer whimpering about my desire for discreet sexual encounters, but had broken through to, like, "What do you fucking mean our session is over bitch? Do I look fucking done to you?"

But it has all made me a better person. The junk. The poppy. It like brings out my best. Now I wink, give a thumbs up, and say "thank you" to the lifeguards on my way up to the showers.

In the train station, after I almost nodded out, I walked to the pubic men's room, and as I arrived this woman was awkwardly trying to push a man in a wheelchair through the door. First I sort of held the door for her, but she didn't want to go in, since, as I said, it was the men's room. So I offered to push the wheelchair in for her, while she waited outside. Then the door closed and I was like all alone with this old corpse with like no legs, and like…what was I gonna do? Like bear-hug the stranger from behind and hold him up in front of the urinal?

27

So I went back out and told her that maybe she should go in and take care of him and that I would, like, commandeer things. I was in charge. All dilated and up, even while half asleep. No peripheral vision whatsoever. "Everyone has to leave the men's room at once!" I instructed. And I stood guard. And she was grateful. And I guess the guy in the wheelchair was too—I don't know. He never moved a muscle really.

And I was standing outside the closed door and this plump Mexican guy holding a children's guitar in a cardboard box who had just witnessed my leadership, looked me deep in the eyes with glowing admiration and said, "You are a very nice man."

II

The brain

of a wrinkled poet was finally mine. The brain had once sat in a skull in a head on the same park bench every day. For forty years. Now, finally, this brain was mine.

It was like a black glove with mini-marbles in the knuckles and fingers. I tried to pin down its octopussial tentacles and rub the hard little satin-covered nodules. (These are the calcified ideas. Original ideas. Content.)

The poet had published three collections and had managed to have them all graduate from print into oblivion. Impressive.

When he wasn't on his bench in the park, he was in a bare studio apartment, furnished with just a window. The fresh light was baked daily. And a royal blue sleeping bag occupied the floor like man's best friend.

And there was one other odd accessory: a huge iron crowbar, that sat on the floor next to the bed. It was there in the event of a cave-in.

I probed further, using my micro-scalpel and digital arthroscope to make an incision, and remove one of the ideas, which I was then able to examine more closely under a high-powered lens. It looked like a pink peppercorn. I tapped it lightly with my mallet. It didn't crumble. When I pinched it with my forceps, I found it far less brittle than I had anticipated. It was more like an egg of caviar in layered, compressed plates of zinc armor. It was a complex BB with callouses. A caper of flesh. I took it and peeled it like a microscopic cabbage—removing one layer after the next.

Each leaf had a rather pronounced network of vessels branching across its moth-like surface. The vessels were bulging like the veins on the back of my hand.

I picked up

my daughter, Cole, from school and she asked if we could go with the other kids over to Cadman Plaza.

Cole ran off to play, and I walked along the row of park benches under the budding trees, looking for a place to park myself. That was when I met this cute Japanese babysitter, whose name I now forget. To be honest, she kind of flagged me down, pointing out the free seat next to her.

I finally took a good look at my new Japanese friend. As pretty as she was, it was her neat hoodie that really caught my eye. "Um, is that a Kusama?" I asked, politely.

She nodded and smiled. I looked away for a second and then back at her boyish chest, fixating my eyes on the trippy, yellow cartoony…um…something. It was either a bright yellow gourd or a bright yellow octopus rendered in Kusama's ubiquitous vocabulary of graphic dots.

"I really like your hoodie," I said. I must have really been moved, because I continued with the invasive question that I normally don't stoop so low to ask: "Where did you get it?"

"Uniqlo," she answered. "It was on sale."

Yikes. Maybe Yayoi Kusama was destined to be printed on the front of a hoodie, the way Hokusai's *The Great Wave* was meant for the mug.

Canvas never was Kusama's best ground. Look at the absurd dots she once painted on the surface of a living horse. And have you ever seen the quickly dissolving dots she painted on a pond. She waded in naked with a can of paint and a brush.

The other day was

my wife Cory's birthday and we decided to have a family dinner down the hill at our neighborhood restaurant. I dragged my clan across the street, and we made our way down the steep hill under a canopy of cherry blossoms.

Two blocks and we came to the restaurant's sweet little affordable menu posted in a giant plate glass window. I held my hand up to the window to block the reflection and peeked in. To my delight, the dining room was basically empty. By some miracle we'd beaten the Sunday evening crowd, which is hard to do these days, ever since my charming, low-key neighborhood became a tourist destination.

Our panoramic view of Manhattan is now blocked by a new condo and a hotel eclipses much of the Brooklyn Bridge. And the view we once had going all the way up to the

Chrysler Building is no more. Now, if you turn your head to the right, you're staring at the plumber's crack of a crappy condo that says: I'm just gonna squeeze right in here and stand in front of you and watch the sunset.

As we eased in through the front door, relieved to be seconds away from an ice-cold Peroni, we were greeted, more halted, by a hostess, who stepped up to me. "We would be happy to seat you back there," she said in a thick Italian accent, turning towards the restaurant's dark back section, which I already knew to be the place they kept things like a mop and bucket, a wall-mounted cash machine, and a stack of hard plastic booster seats.

I was about to blow my stack. I looked at my "happy family Hunan style." (We've been calling ourselves this ever since reading a dish with this name in a Chinese menu). Then I turned back to the hostess. My pulse was now like the mechanized thumping of a rave. "Um, there are like six open tables here, and—let me count 1, 2, 3, 4, 5—five empty stools at the bar. May we please be seated somewhere up front?" I could vaguely remember the place a few years earlier when the location's previous occupants were selling Twinkies and Lotto tickets from a cat-infested corner in the armpit of the BQE.

I thought about how charmed I was to discover that the place had been turned into a cool little off-the-beaten-path restaurant. I remembered the times I'd sat up at the bar, fantasizing about switching professions and becoming a Hollywood location scout. The view is one of the most captivating street scenes in all of Brooklyn or Manhattan—a "double fall line," as my dad used to call it on the ski slopes.

A feast, not of food, but of a fairytale city—as the blue sky gets darker and bluer and darker and bluer, and the moon and the street lamps dim, and...well, it's called a romantic atmosphere.

Just the Hunan Style Atmosphere I had in mind for Cory's 46th! I scanned the restaurant again, from the bar seats, to the window seats, to the uninviting shadow in the back room, where presumably there was a great big table just waiting for us. Then I looked back at the hostess. By now, the restaurant's single waitress, who must have sensed the confrontation forming, had joined her co-worker in solidarity.

"What's going on here?" I asked. "Are you really holding all of these tables?"

The hostess reached for a little spiral pad and began flipping pages, pretending to count names.

"Don't try to pull that reservation trick on me!" I shouted, as I turned to my daughter and wife, who nodded in agreement. And like the start of a dance in a Broadway musical, we locked elbows, and stepped out in unison, back onto the cobblestone corner.

I was

downtown near J&R Music World, crossing the street, slipping through a narrow gap between a parked mail truck and a parked car, when the truck sounded a repetitive beep and began to inch backwards. I was a few inches from being pinned between two bumpers when I leapt out of harm's way and walked up to the mail truck's open sliding door, and yelled in at the driver: "Watch out man, you almost fucking ran me over!"

"Why don't YOU watch out?" the mailman replied.

Anyway, I gave him the finger and continued on my way. As far as I was concerned, that was the end of it.

I had continued on my way around the corner, when I heard the same mailman rev his engine, gun it to the end of the block, and jam on the breaks, right in front of me and a small crowd of people who were waiting at a bus stop. Out came this buff, tattooed black guy, with violence in his eyes. He was literally hopping in place like a boxer about to enter the ring. His navy and gray uniform was tailored to fit the girth of his bulging biceps and thighs.

I looked at the crowd of strangers waiting for the bus and then back at the postman, who was gesturing for me to take the first shot.

Hum, let me see? What does one do in this situation? Middle fingers and fuck you's are given out with such frequency, and yet, never with much consequence. Did I really deserve this?

Luckily at that moment the mailman must have snapped out of it. Without another word, he gathered himself back in his truck, threw the loud stick shift into gear, and sped off.

About a week later, I found myself back down around J&R when, sure enough, I saw the same mailman, this time on foot, kneeling on one knee, with his key in a mailbox.

I must have been feeling exceptionally diplomatic, because I decided to approach him as if I were some kind of head of state or ambassador or something. I figured I'd extend my kindness and offer him an apology for the fuck you and the horrible middle finger.

He recognized me right away, set his bag down, along with a big bundle of letters. And rose to shake my hand. Only it was hands. Plural. I had both palms facing up and extended to him, in one of those ambassadorial double handshakes. He went for one, clasping the grip of my one hand, and pulling me in to bump his shoulder.

I just

deleted all of my friends. 236 of them. I was fed up. Too many hours flipping through photos. Particularly the photos of very attractive students, who I was kind of keeping tabs on. My intern warned me that they can easily detect old pervs combing through their albums.

Facebook. I doubt I'll miss it. But I'm sad to see Pacey go—after our brief rekindling. Pacey was the guy who sat near me back in fourth grade. My eyes would be sneaking peeks at his desk all day long.

He'd draw. And I admired his line. The sharp point of his black-and-orange McDonogh School pencil. From the tiny pink shards of eraser would emerge a convoy of 18-wheelers in profile. His tractor trailers were remarkably accurate. And they were highly detailed. I remember watching Pacey render the hinge on the lid that flips up and down over the vertical chrome exhaust pipe that extends a few feet upward at the rear of the cab. And I remember watching him slowly render the truck's big old horn. He'd draw that glorious truck horn with total devotion.

Years later, in the upper school, Pacey absurdly claimed to be moonlighting as a professional truck driver. And as unbelievable as it sounded, one day it was actually proven to be true.

My team was piled in a school bus on our way to a game across town at Gilman School. We were out on I-495 just before rush hour. The beltway was packed with cars and trucks, and we all inching along in bumper to bumper traffic when we inched up to Pacey, who was up high behind the wheel of a massive rig with a big dip tucked in his bottom lip.

We all jumped up and slid down our windows. A frenzy broke out across the entire bus, and we began to make honking motions like little kids on family road trips. Pacey, cool and poised, glanced over and gave us a little nod. It was hard to see his expression under the severely bent visor of his mesh trucker cap. He reached up and grabbed the chord above his head and pulled down on it, sounding the rig's baritone foghorn.

When I eventually reconnected with Pacey on Facebook, I told him how I had longed to see his fourth grade drawings again. He admitted that he still had one of them. It was hanging in a frame in his office on his ship. He explained that he'd graduated from hauling cargo up and down the New Jersey Turnpike to transporting giant shipping containers across the deep blue sea, where he spent six months of every year away from his wife and kids.

A real poet.

There's

a movie about going into the human mind and erasing memories. And scrubbing a very painful breakup.

Anyway, it's been on my mind lately.

I've been having a similar idea, equally sci-fi and, I guess, mildly surreal. But mine is sort of anti-dystopian.

In my therapy, two very nice people reconnect at a high-school reunion and decide to help each other out. They were never really friends to begin with, nor were they strangers. They were at best familiar with each other.

They agree, in any event, to take part in a correspondence—a contractual agreement to write no less than five-thousand words of nostalgic and explicit false memories about a high-school love affair they never really had. They're instructed to intentionally disregard this fact.

Their back and forth letters eventually form a richly layered narrative about a romance that begins to feel strikingly like a real memory. The result is that both patients kind of brainwash each other into believing that they, in fact, do share a significant coming-of-age encounter, or what I would call, a missed opportunity that wasn't missed, an un-missed opportunity.

My head is

filled with fog. A harbor. Words like flat barges trace slowly past the jagged architecture. Buildings punch the sky like staple guns.

I can't spell. You know that. This makes me mentally retarded. I'm an old-school retard. Meaning simply awkward.

I did a poetry reading the other day for my daughter's fourth grade class. The teacher turned the fan off so my voice could be heard. I began to gush sweat. I'd taken a shower before going over, and I guess I hadn't given my body enough time to cool down. Showers are like rare these days. It's like I was cleaning up for a formal. Fresh boxers and a Beefy-T from deep down in the drawer.

Rather than reading a poem, I got distracted by the overhead projector, which was refracting a golden rectangle onto the wall behind me. I remember when Mel, our lower school janitor, would come in and erase the enormous slate chalkboards. The gray-tone would turn black behind his damp sponge.

I tried to explain that poets hear things. That we're "homonymially challenged."

One smart kid asked, "How many books have you sold?" My answer: "Just a few." I smiled. She assumed I was kidding.

But none of this is up to me. A future is fishing for me. But unable to hook me. It can't find me. It can't bait me. It can't time itself with my time to feed.

It's a future that seems to pull so many along in its lively net. A future trolling and leaving a persistent wake for all the world to admire.

I arrived at

the gate as my flight was boarding and headed straight to the counter, where I confronted the agent. "I have a little problem," I said, trying not to lose my shit. "I checked in online on my way over in the cab, and there weren't any more aisle seats."

"It's a very full flight," the agent replied, staring blankly into the abyss of her monitor. "But let me see what I can do for you."

I watched the blue glare of her computer flicker in her oversized, non-prescription glasses, as she tapped noisily on her plastic keyboard.

She was one of the fashionable, overly educated hipsters to, in recent years, reclaim the term *stewardess*. It had become almost a form of method acting, for women, that is, in their early twenties, to get jobs with major airlines in order to receive decent salaries, while reviving a certain glamorous 70s lifestyle with various fringe benefits.

I turned around to be sure no one was in line behind me adding to the pressure I was putting on the poor agent, and I looked across the room at the last few passengers as they handed their tickets to the other hipster agent and boarded.

My agent and me were now the only two people remaining at the gate. (By the way, many people are not aware that it is customary for the agent to board the plane and become the flight attendant.)

"Can I see your ID?" she asked politely.

I gave her my driver's license and begged her again for an aisle seat. I've grown accustomed to begging for things, in general. I've become needy in so many ways. But my single most essential requirement when flying (or riding buses) was, and still is, an aisle seat. And there is a good reason for my dependency: namely, my bladder.

A single beer at high altitude causes my bladder to drop the ball. In a three-hour flight, I'm likely to get up from my seat, destroy the peace and relaxation of anyone unlucky enough to be blocking me in, and head to the bathroom at the back of the plane. This can happen anywhere between six and ten times. It really does get quite repetitive.

One time, even when the "fasten your seat belt" light was lit and the plane was bouncing all over the place, "encountering turbulence," as they say, I unclasped my metal seatbelt, squeezed out past my neighbor, and stumbled like a Parkinson's patient down the narrow aisle to the bathroom. On my way, I passed row after row of attentive faces who I'm sure saw me as your basic bedwetter. I locked myself in, peed for however many minutes, and flushed. Only, rather than washing up and returning to my seat, I continued to stand in front of the toilet with my zipper down, and my penis out, listening to the hum, shifting my weight, as if trying to keep my balance on a snowboard, and feeling my bladder refill until the point when it was ready to empty out a second time.

To be honest, I no longer find it embarrassing to talk about any of this. I'm perfectly willing to explain my situation to any of the agents of the world. I don't try to hide my vulnerabilities, especially from gorgeous college-age women. The fact that I'm, like, "geriatric at 40" is probably the best thing I have going.

I've come to realize at this stage of midlife that I feel more and more like I'm suffering from early-onset-elderliness. And any confession about this feeling is like ammo. It's what keeps me feeling fully alive.

Some people jump into frigid lakes in places like Green Bay, Wisconsin in the middle of the winter, whereas I try to give everyone around me an opportunity to laugh at me.

So what if a hipster with giant eyes behind giant dark-rimmed glasses sees me as an old timer in a diaper? So what?

Basically, I'm hard up for humor. I'm desperate for the intoxication of a little LOL. I'd rather receive a quick bolt of irreversible humiliation than be obliged to keep up some kind of mannequin disposition all day.

If I were NOT one to offer up my daily experiences as the subject matter of ongoing comic relief, I'd be tricking everyone into thinking that I actually think highly of myself!

In truth, I have such low self-esteem, such a deflated ego, such guilt, such interplanetary negativity, so many character flaws, such a borderline personality disorder, such bad fucking karma, so much built up toxicity and rage, that it kind of makes sense for me to just go with it. Rather than feeling caught up in some one else's suspicion that I may be unfit to participate in whatever "group activity" awaits us, it makes far more sense for me to embody the spirit of the "pisser."

"Do you have a small bladder?" the agent asked.

"Small?"

She rephrased the question. "Would you say you have a diminished bladder?"

"I'm not sure." It was the first time I wondered if having a small bladder was like another of these typical male lacks.

"I'm just kidding," the agent said, cracking a very charming smile. "It happens to a lot of passengers," she reassured me. "It's very common. Especially with the heavy drinkers on board."

I'm not really such a heavy drinker, I thought.

"You do have a drinking problem, don't you?"

"Yes, I guess I do," I said, wondering to myself, as always, how on earth one beer can could possibly have enough fluid ounces in it to continuously fill and refill my bladder so many times consecutively.

The agent looked up at me, comparing my face with the far more youthful face pictured under the creased and scratched lamination of my New York State driver's license, which was going on its third decade. The thing actually was starting to look like my first fake ID that I made at Kinko's in ninth grade. It is indeed odd that my ID had expired and been renewed now multiple times without requiring an up-to-date photo. The photo truly was a childhood picture, and thus confusing, to say the least.

"I see you grew a beard," she said, looking back at the picture of a cleanly shaven twenty-something on my ID. She glared back into her computer, and began to mumble under her breath: "mature…it makes you look more mature." She mouthed the word "mature," as if she were rehearsing to go live with the word.

"I wouldn't actually call this a beard," I said, tugging at a few springy hairs, feeling them extend slightly away from my face, knowing damn well that I looked like a cousin of Richard Reid, aka the Shoe Bomber. It's just, you know, a little growth.

"Ok, so its not a beard, it's just…"

"Extended stubble," I shot back, pleased with the quality of the flirtation we were having. "I wasn't in the mood to shave."

"All year? Look, just own it man! Own your "old-man" beard. Own your bush. I own my bush!

"Your bush?"

"Yeah. You better believe it. I own my bush."

I laughed, totally pleased with my new friend's audacity. I was now becoming concerned that we were about to miss our flight.

"You look like a cartoonist," she said, continuing to treat me with unprecedented unprofessionalism. "Are you a cartoonist?"

"A cartoonist?"

"Yes. Are you a cartoonist?"

"No. I'm not a cartoonist. Why do you ask?"

The agent laughed. "You know there is something that is very good for men who demand aisle seats.

"Yeah? What?"

"Ecstasy. You know, molly."

"Really?"

"Yeah, that's what we all use."

"Who's *we all*?"

"Us flight attendants. Try releasing your bladder when you're on ecstasy. It's virtually impossible."

"I've never done ecstasy. I wouldn't know."

"Guess what?" the agent said, looking up from her screen with her remarkable meaty smile. "You're in luck! We have one vacant seat left for you. It's the last seat in the very back of the plane."

"Wonderful!"

"You will have your own totally private section."

"Private?"

"I can offer you one of the toilets." Somehow the agent managed to keep a straight face. "But remember there's positively no smoking or vaping in there!"

"I don't smoke or vape," I said, with equal mono-tonal flatness. It was now pretty clear, my new friend did not see me as geriatric, but as an "older man," and we were actually hitting it off. Before the end of the flight, I bargained, I'd be typing my email address into her cell phone and sending myself an email with the single word "Hi."

"I'm just kidding. I have a seat for you in row 12," she said, as she proudly handed me a fresh ticket with a big 12B printed across it.

"Oh my god! This is great!" I said, "Thank you so much!"

"I'll be on the flight too," she said. "So I'll come by and check on you, OK?"

I looked down at her American Airlines pin that read Julie Dodge. And together we walked down the ramp and boarded the plane.

Moments later we were airborne on our way to Boston's Logan International Airport. I was deep in thought about the talk I was scheduled to give at the ICA later that evening based on the theme of Love. I still wasn't sure what to say about Love. I hadn't written anything down. Jenelle had reassured me that we'd just chat the same way we do on the phone about whatever comes to mind. "But what if nothing comes

48

to mind?" I thought, knowing that my ideas about love and romance were not exactly heart-warming for anyone but me. I mean, I had this idea that love is about planting a seed. And the seed, you see, grows. Sometimes slowly. Sometimes quickly. A woman, no matter how old, no matter how happily married, no matter how wealthy, and with however many kids, will lay in bed with my little book of poems on her night-stand. She will wake up in the middle of the night, with her husband asleep in bed next to her, and she'll stuff pillows under her sheet, and sneak out of the house, and come to me.

"Hello? HELLO? Are you there?" It was the agent, my agent, Julie Dodge, who was now playing stewardess. She'd come down the aisle pushing the beverage cart, preparing to fill drink orders. She reached past me handing a small cup of ice and a can of diet ginger ale to my neighbor. He thanked her and politely went back to staring out the window.

Julie then set a bottled water down on my tray stand, along with a cocktail napkin. Then her hand returned to the nap-kin, placing upon it a single pink and green capsule.

I looked up at her, catching her eyes which were filled with warmth and excitement. Her neck was wrapped in her red American Airlines silk scarf. Her dark hair was now pulled back in a neat bun. Her dark-rimmed hipster glasses contin-ued to offer concentrated intelligence. Her eyes were flickering like tiny birthday candles. She then came closer to my ear and whispered, "I already took mine."

III

I met

up with my old secretary, Alyse, last night for a few beers. We were headed down the crowded sidewalk, when I asked, "Can we, like, find a place to dictate? The way we used to? I feel like I have a good one in me."

"Where?" she asked.

"In me! I don't know—in my brain? Just in me. In my nervous system, I guess? In my breath?"

"No, you idiot! I mean where do you want to go to dictate the poem?"

"How about right here?" I suggested, stepping to the side to let the river of pedestrians rush by. "How about if you type it into your phone?"

To my great satisfaction, Alyse then took out her phone and nodded for me to begin, at which point, frantic words sort of spilled out like a basket of brand-new tennis balls. "Ok, so way back…like a while ago…I met this much younger woman…who was also teaching a painting class for one semester…and like we went out one night in the city…

after my best friend's opening down on the Lower East Side…his first big opening…it was like in a past life…"

"Could you slow down?" Alyse cut in. "I'm out of practice."

"Ok, I'm sorry," I said, smiling in a way that acknowledged just how self-centered I was being, while giving myself full poetic license to continue. Alyse shot me a look, which seemed to say: you better make this worth my while, and then got back in character.

"So, anyway, I tried to get her to sympathize with me…"

Alyse stopped typing. I could tell she was judging me. I went on. "I told this much younger painter I was really jealous of my friend's success as a painter, and that basically I wanted to enlist her to take part in a kind of special operation. I could not get myself to go to his show, I explained, unless I too had something to show."

"And…"

"And she said 'Yes!' She actually said 'Yes.' And keep in mind, she had already declined my two previous invitations. I'm not sure why she agreed to do it. I think she may have felt sorry for me. The same way she pitied her boyfriend who had, like…a stutter."

"A what?"

"A stutter!" I repeated, feeling a wave of excitement smack down across the beach. "I'm not making this up. He had a fucking stutter! A really bad stutter! I'm not kidding, Alyse!"

Alyse chuckled, as she typed in the word s-t-u-t-t-e-r, before quickly returning to her formal deadpan expressionless expression.

Now my poem had humor! It had personality! I had something. I was psyched. I continued: "A few nights later, my muse—I'm just gonna go ahead and call her my muse, OK?…a few nights later, we met near the steps up onto the pedestrian walkway of the Brooklyn Bridge and we headed across to Manhattan to attend the opening. We walked at a pretty good pace, side by side, bundled in our winter layers, passed by the occasional bicyclist. My hands were shoved in my pockets, and hers were in her gloves—the same gloves (the ones with the fingertips cut off) that she had on when I first struck up a conversation with her in the faculty lounge.

"My muse really came through for me. She stood near me in the crowded gallery, challenging the room full of paintings with just her blue eyes." I gave Alyse a second to catch up with me. "She stood around with me chitchatting pretty much with whomever I was chitchatting with. And when our entourage moved on to the private dinner, she stayed by my side, burning with contained energy every step of the way. Soon we were seated next to each other at a long table somewhere on the Lower East Side, and she continued to stick out just the way I wanted her to stick out. Together we stole a little bit of the spotlight. I think people were marveling at the audacity of bringing along a mysterious muse in place of Cory, who was adored by many of the people at the event.

"Finally the dinner came to an end, and a bunch of us headed off to some bar on the Bowery. And my muse stayed on and really went the distance with me, sitting up at the bar with me away from the rest of the pack who sat across the room at some table. After a few hours, I looked over and they were gone. My best friend didn't even bother to say goodnight. Perhaps he was pissed at me for stealing that one little ray of his spotlight?"

Alyse's face was glowing in the radiance of her phone, happy to be getting my poem down, helping me deposit my words in the bank. A lively flow of urbanites continued to parade past us. She nodded for me to continue.

"Eventually we woke up in the back of a cab. Some of our clothes were undone or completely off. I remember the driver's tan face in the rearview mirror, as he politely informed us, in his gentle Pakistani voice, that the meter was running."

Alyse cracked a smile.

"I peeked over the seat at the meter. It read $267 and something!"

"Jesus."

"I know. And I was totally bewildered. I looked out the window and I have to say, I had no idea what neighborhood we were even in. But I felt great. My last memory was of our lips kind of bumping together with each shock of the cab's cushion as we sped back across the Brooklyn Bridge. I remember how braided towels of light lashed the windows until there was no longer any strength in our necks or eyelids or tongues."

Alyse lifted her eye from her lit-up device. They were bright and full of approval. Whenever something even remotely erotic happened in one of my poems, her face would soften and her gaze would sort of become erect. This would naturally encourage me to go deeper in my confession.

"A few months later, my muse informed me that she had lost her studio and that she needed a place to paint and live.

56

I figured I'd help her push onward in her spartan existence. She always had this thermos full of hot tea. Tea was her three-meals-a-day. And the thermos seemed to be her only real possession, except for her paint brushes and stuff. So I gave her the keys to my room in Dumbo."

"You let her use your office?"

"Well yes. Alyse, you have to realize, I had stopped going. The room was just sitting there vacant. The place was just too lonely. But I was still paying rent. There was a desk and a chair in there. And, I think, a pair of faded A.P.C. jeans hanging on the wall (which I had at one point considered an artwork), and maybe a broom. I told her she could stay there for about a year in exchange for a small painting. When we shook on it, I felt her gloved hand, but without the grip of her naked fingertips. I had been downgraded. Now I guess I was little more than a landlord and critic."

"Did you say 'critic?'"

"I stopped by once to check on her, which is when I saw her injured cheerleaders all over the wall."

"Her what? She was painting cheerleaders?"

"INJURED cheerleaders! One time, I remember sitting in the room sipping a hot cup of tea that she kept filling from her thermos, as I tried to articulate what I thought of those cheerleaders, which were painted in a cartoony, anachronistic, vaguely Bruegel-ish style. Not to my surprise, the series of small oil paintings that were completed over the next few months became her first big New York solo show. Which promptly sold out! I was invited to the opening. But of course, I opted out. At this point, I was on lockdown, and my lust for life had become a bust for life."

Alyse tilted her head, as if to say, "You deserved far worse."

"And things just kept going up and up and up for my painter muse. Soon she dumped her stuttering boyfriend, and other acquaintances. And her teaching gig. And she dumped my charity and my criticism. She dumped the whole city really. And moved back to Canada to paint her heart out.

"The other day I came across a review of her work on some art blog. She'd moved on from injured cheerleaders to lonely, aproned women peeling carrots. That's when it hit me that we had never completed our trade. In fact, I had forgotten all about it.

"One of her paintings would surely be worth something now! She had collectors, after all, and a market. Some day, I thought, my daughter will be able to put her kid through college with that little painting. I had to make it happen. I had to act. It was my responsibility to my family.

"So I got up my nerve and sent my old muse an email reminding her of our trade and asking that she be so kind to pick one out and send it to me. And about three months later, a package arrived at my door with her name and Canadian return address written in the top left corner. I thanked the UPS driver and tripped up the stairs with excitement. I grabbed a knife and cut open the top of the box and ripped apart a layer of bubble wrap. I gently eased my sweet little Bruegel-ish oil painting from the wrapper. I flipped it over. It was signed.

"The painting was not of an injured cheerleader or a lonely woman peeling a carrot. It was totally different. I imagined that it was a painting of us. In it, a bearded old guy stands behind his young female student at her easel, studying the painting she is working on.

"I stood there in my tranquil apartment lost in the painting for some time, occasionally glancing around the room trying to decide which wall to hang it on. But I couldn't hang it. What would Cory say? She'd certainly want to know who painted it. And where it came from. And I'd have to tell her. And we'd then have to go through the whole thing again. The thing about poetry and love and stuff. I slid the canvas back into its cardboard box and taped it shut. I took a Sharpie and blacked out the return address, so as to hide the sender's name from anyone who might discover it in the future. I took it into my bedroom and shoved it as deep as I could into the back of my closet."

I google

Eric P. Dollard. He's at his usual spot, in the front seat of his 1978 Mazda, parked under a power line. His door is open. His front door. He's giving yet another interview to another fan. He speaks with a Tucson drawl, explaining how Tesla's patents allow us to harness electrical energy straight from the ether without producing heat. Through the car's stereo he listens to the gulp and gurgle of the earth's core.

He's a non-conformist. Like that other electrical engineer who was put away by Reagan after designing a motor that could run all day on a single can of Dr. Pepper. I love pseudoscience. I love it!

Next time I read my work in public, I'm gonna cut out big cardboard letters and paint them red. I'm gonna prop them up behind me: T-E-D. Pseudoscientists get all the fans.

They get all the love letters—for viral YouTubes of levitating beer cans. The Pseudos get all the attention. They go viral. Unlike poets.

If I post a poem—this poem—and check in the morning to see how many views I get, I bet I'll find zero. I'm afraid to post. I know I won't get a single solitary view. I know it. I know I'm only this one single solitary human. I'm not viewed.

I felt

secure for a brief moment, as I pondered Plan B. And Plan C. And the augmented Plan A. Three plans. Plan A is to get a hustle. Apply to become clergy at the Universal Ministry and perform marriage ceremonies for rosy Republicans in their twenties. I see free drinks in this. And the occasional one that would get away. Me, that is. Getting away. With murder. Or, there's the radio show. Remember that idea? I'll need someone to be my Robin. And someone to be my Baba Booey. I'll go on live every night around 2:00 am and speak in a mellow voice. The same voice as now. The same voice you hear in these words. And I'll help those who call in, desperate from their struggle in the Art World. I'll hear those bitter art handlers and the anorexic gallery chicks paid to fluff up the collector prior to the big bad Zwirner. Plan B: a new life. A completely new life. Far far away. Where I'll work for a low wage at a home for old age. I'll wear yellow plastic clogs. No one will recognize me. No one will spot me. Unless, by chance, some old Minimalist happens to get dumped there. Lawrence Weiner. Plan C. This one is totally risky. It calls for selling the art books. And the Gibson. And the futon. And living on algae shakes.

I ordered

a four-thousand dollar Gibson arch-top hollow-body on line. And it came today in a cardboard box. And the UPS woman handed me her digital pad and I signed, and after she pulled off in her truck, I stood for a second with my box at my front door. Rather than rushing upstairs, ripping it open, and plugging it into my amp, I decided to carry the box two blocks around the corner to the UPS store, where I filled out a shipping invoice, and left it to be sent back to the factory. Round trip.

Why? Why did I balk? The guitar, I realized, did not fit my disposition. It was new. And I was old. It was perfect and I was imperfect. It was expensive and I was cheap. I imagined myself holding it balanced on my knee. I imagined seeing myself reflected in the dark stain of its shellacked body and pristine ebony pick-guard.

Then all I could think was how many hollow-bodies and semi-hollow bodies get manufactured and shipped out every day to middle-aged men just like me who can't play like Joe Pass and never will.

I miss my

Boston Acoustics. I remember the salesman who sold me the twin blocks. Those boutique audio guys were such goons.

Maybe I could get my speakers back. And go into sound therapy. And work from home. And have patients. Maybe I can get them to come right here to my bedroom. I could play music. The way Weinstock used to do it. He'd cough out a bong hit and crank up Derek and the Dominoes and, like, stand in front of me making eyebrow shapes while pretending to bend up guitar strings. Strings of air.

Today is another research day for me. Being a Freudian, my research is, um, dreaming. So I'll have no choice but to drop my pen and take a nap. Tomorrow I'll work on my poem. (There—I've penciled it in.) I plan to get back to the one I've been working on: the one with no words, just vibrations, denoted by somehow scientifically charting the force of each propulsive wave as it leaves the diaphragm before it reaches the vocal chords. A wordless, and soundless poem. A poem that is purely the will to create a sound.

When I was

playing football in maybe sixth grade, I slipped through a narrow gap between the tackle and guard and found myself with some running room. I was on my way, when my knees were swept out from under me. The whistle blew and the ball was dead at the one yard line.

Turns out I had torn the anterior cruciate of my right knee. What was I feeling? Pain? Not really. Disappointment? No. Quite the contrary. Relief.

But why? With or without an injury, why hadn't some force, some momentum—some fight!—carried me one more yard? Had some part of my drive been drained out? Extruded?

Even had I been decapitated by my chin strap when the freckled tackler Alfie Weedman took me down, wouldn't my zombie arm have reached out and out…and wouldn't I have been rescued by…by Conquest?

You'd think. Right? But I now see that my monstrous unreliable ligament had a mind of its own that day. My leg had a subversive agenda. It was a symptom of my repressed desire, my stubborn desire, to continue to live in a malleable fantasy.

My knee simply would not carry me over that hurdle. My body would not propel me beyond that significant comfort into the terminal "zone of end." The End Zone!

And to this day, I remain touchdown-less. I remain something of a dreamer, looking back to that fated day. It is my conviction that I experienced a kind of ecstatic shut down. An ACL orgasm. An involuntary ejaculation of my ligament into the fleshy socket of my knee. Alfie had not tackled me so much as embraced my collapse, padded my fall. Padded me! From overwhelming expectations.

Sillman

was gaining weight. He was straining to keep up his Albers impersonation. He was bulging through his grayish blue sweater. And his pleated tan pants were extending with his waistline. But it was his starched white dress shirt that held his Albers costume together.

63

His color class had become a kind of theater piece, based on his own studies with the man himself, Josef Albers. Sillman had memorized like every Albers class he'd ever been in and could do them with precision over a twelve-week semester. He had been doing it over and over again for at least twenty years. Most people I'm sure had no idea that he was a total actor. All those Black Mountain guys were long gone. Who was gonna call him out on it?

When a semester would end, he'd take a little break, get his pill-y wool sweater dry-cleaned, his slacks pressed, and his white shirt starched and then get right back to it. He'd even wear his sweater in the warm months. I always thought, "Take that thing off man. I'm getting hot just looking at you."

Sillman used some sort of product in his side-parted silver hair. Did I mention that? He had that sort of Albers shell. Very tidy. Albers "cleaned up nicely," to use a term Harry Chapin's sexy daughter once used on me. She said it when she saw me walk into the wedding in a tux. (Time out. I have to address this: I was the only one in a tux! Neither the groom nor his father were in a tux. Just me and the caterers. So I called Frog—who is an old-school WASP—and I said, "Frog, I'm here with Cory. Picture a wedding invitation on 100% cotton with the italic word *formal* emboss-printed right above the RSVP line. What does that mean?" And Frog's reply: "Black tie." Black fucking tie. Good.

I charged back inside, directly across the dance floor, to the bar, and back to the daughter of the dead folk singer.

Anyway, after I got through with the Sillman color class I sort of buried the experience in my memory—I had no use for it till now. And now here I am thinking about this shit. I buried it all away. I buried away the cool exercises we did. The one where we made one color look like two colors; and another one where we made two colors look like one color. It was so scientific! That's what I want to do one day—teach color in a science school. That's what made Albers so cool. Science is like so friggin' cool.

I'm building a Tesla coil right now that will energize my home, and cure all the cancer in my like entire neighborhood, not to mention the anti-missile defense it will provide to all of downtown Manhattan. The new Freedom Tower, which is visible out my window, looks like a baby's braided birthday candle tonight. I type. I close my eyes.

Sillman also got us drawing the way Albers drew. And the way Albers taught students to draw. We spent like three or four consecutive weeks with ellipses drawn from the deep study of the top of an empty flower pot, which had been set out on the table, where it would appear to hover. Other classes got naked models, or extravagant still lives with like dead trout. Not in Sillman's Color Theory class. We just had to sit with this boring flower pot. There wasn't even a flower in it.

The idea was to hold the pencil to the paper and concentrate on the ellipse and, like, just let go. No sketchy unsure lines. No hesitant arks. Just fluid circles. At evenly tempered angles. If the ellipse was drawn correctly, then, and only then, would the space of the page open into an illusion of a third dimension.

Sillman would work his way around the room critiquing our work. He'd bend over the back of each student to get a closer look. When he got to me, I felt him lean in and poke me with his bouncy-ball front. And then his white sausage fingers would gently take my tight claw and hold my hand as we drew together. As molesting as this was—and it was—I have to admit it worked. Through his guidance I quickly got a feel for it.

Did Albers do this? Did he draw with the hands of his students at Yale? And at Black Mountain College? And at the Bauhaus? Did he draw till they drew the rim of gorgeous ceramic flowerpots on creamy gray newsprint?

He must have.

So much is happening all at

once. The earth is spinning. And I'm drinking a cup of tea. See? Two things! At once!

Let's step down into the spinning world, as light glitters through the tympanic drum of my skull. The Stock Exchange is desolate on Sunday. The ferry docks, and we step right on. I love telling people "thank you" these days. Workers. I try to grab their attention that way. A pat on the back to the players on my team.

Which is not to say that there is anything friendly about me. See me part the parading Diabetes people on the Brooklyn Bridge, yelling, "Coming through!" and making my arms into a wedge.

I even hurled Cole's Razor scooter at a Mercedes Benz, and I chucked Hoke's little plastic poop bag at a cab as it sped by.

At lunch I told Hugh about my screenplay. "It's a wedding movie," I told him: "KC and his band have become like this super in-demand wedding band. They are big-time snackers, and heavy boozers. They play all their hits, brilliantly. But everyone thinks they are just a cover band. Who'd imagine that they were the actual KC and the Sunshine Band? So anyway, the bride doesn't want to leave the party. She's having too much fun. The groom eventually goes up to sleep. As has happened to so many other boyfriends in the past, he pays the price for being romantically involved with a binger. Keep in mind, they haven't consummated their marriage. The bride goes off and gets lost back in the kitchen searching for the leftovers from dinner which have been put away in the walk-in refrigerator. While back there, she runs into KC, who is also "getting into the trash" as they say. They each snack, snort a few lines of Coke off one of the steel industrial kitchen tables, and fall into a long talk that ends in a long, very sensuous kiss. When the band regroups for the last set, they play my favorite slow dance, "Babe, I love you so, I want you to know. Please don't go…" (give that a second. Let it soak in.) The bride and KC dance and hug and kiss again and the song ends for the ten or eleven remaining guests who then witness another wedding on the spot officiated in a haze of cold beers and leftover bite-size crab cakes."

IV

The girl got

into the pool, as I was finishing lap one-hundred. She was standing in the shallow end in my lane adjusting her goggles. While turning I came up really close to her, in her skull-tight bathing cap. The next time down she was doing a kind of hamstring stretch. And the next time, it was her muscular back that caught my attention.

She started swimming breaststroke, so I decided to switch from crawl and to also swim breaststroke. My goal was to arrive at my wall and turn just as she was turning at the opposite end. If I timed it right, we'd both swim towards one another and pass in the middle of the pool. How else was I gonna get to spend some time with this girl?

Each time we passed, there was a frozen moment. It was so awkward. It must have gone on for twenty or thirty laps. I wanted to believe that she was, at the very least, aware of my awareness of her. Even though she gave no indication, I wanted to believe this.

After around the 130th lap, I turned around to start lap 131, and she was gone. That quickly, she had gotten out of the pool, toweled off, slipped into her sandals, and escaped up the wet stairs.

So I finished my next lap and, the thrill being gone, also got out of the pool—sacrilegiously. It was an odd number. I never finished on an odd number.

I saw the girl again a few days later. She was once again in my lane, preparing to swim, doing her usual hamstring stretch. This time when I swam into make my turn, I did what we swimmers probably shouldn't confess to doing: I took about a second to study her body under the water.

Maybe a day or two later, there we were again. Both swimming, and I'd like to think enjoying each other's company. She paused to stretch. I wondered if her stretching was an intentional way to create an opportunity for me to study her body under water. Or perhaps it was even a way to create an opportunity for us to meet?

I thought it through, deciding that indeed, she was stretching, delaying, so that I'd talk to her. It was time to act. If I didn't act I'd be a chicken.

I began to rehearse, inviting her out for a drink in my mind. I stopped swimming and stood next to her, pretending to catch my breath and adjust my goggles. Rings of water formed around my waist. I'd meet her outside on the sidewalk with wet hair and we'd walk down the street…we'd go for vodka! Right. For vodka. I was ready to ask the girl if she'd like to get a vodka, but I lost my nerve.

When would the next opportunity come? A few days later. She was stretching in my lane when I finally decided to take a huge chance. Rather than turn and continue, I pulled over and waited with her. I was kind of crowding her. I let the other two swimmers pass us, so that we'd have a second of privacy. I pulled up my goggles, and looked at her. Her head was capped and her eyes were shielded by mirrored goggles, and most of her body was submerged in the water. It was virtually impossible to determine her age. Was she twenty? Thirty? Forty? That was when I blurted out my best autistic "Hi."

She looked at me, like, I think, to see if there was anyone looking after me. And then she actually smiled, cutely, and pushed off the wall, disappearing in front of a strong kick. There was a *Something About Mary*-ish vibe to the whole thing. But hey! Let's hear it for me! I broke the ice.

I saw her a few days later and decided to play it cool. To play hard-to-get. She was a few lanes down. I could have sworn she kind of waved at me. But I couldn't be sure. I pulled up my goggles, and said, "Did I say hi to you the other day?"

And she answered with obvious confusion "Um…a… yeah. I think you did." I thought her face warmed up to me at that moment, which seems to have caused these words to shoot out of my mouth. "Well…hi again."

"Hi again," she said, kind of mimicking me.

"When we're done swimming, um, would you like to go get a v-v-v-v-v-v-"

"A what?"

"A v-v-v-v-v-v-vod-vod-"

"A vodka?"

"Yes, a vodka."

73

No was her answer. Just no. She simply said, "No." Not even "No thanks." She turned and swam off.

All that pain for nothing.

Ugh

Where do these three letters come from? U-g-h. Onomatopoeia. Good word. Charlie Brown taught me that word. But the best words are homonyms. No? The best words, at least for me, are homonyms. But I'm like poorly wired. I still mouth out words.

Anyway, did I tell you what happened at the supermarket? The cashier was like staring closely at the signature on my Mastercard with this really suspicious look on her face. And she then asked me to sign again. (By the way, I hadn't yet bothered to peel off the "please activate your card" sticker, which I think may have added to her suspicion. It's been three years that I've been using the card with that sticker on it.)

"A signature," I told her, "is not a fingerprint. It isn't proof I am who I say I am. My signature is just me giving you my word. It doesn't identify or not identify me, you fucking idiot!"

I was being obnoxious. She was doing her best. But this somewhat menace is what a writer must be. At all times. The guy who leaves the sticker on his card.

I just bought a printer. After weeks of contemplation. I had to prepare my mind for the incoming machine. This is my creative process. Bracing for a horrible decision that will stick.

When it arrives in the UPS truck, in the next few days, I know what will happen. I will rush upstairs. I will take it out of the box. I will hook it up, (without reading the directions). And finally, I will print out my poem. In Courier. So the poem will appear as if it had been typed on an IBM typewriter in the 50s. And this being the case, I would be made to feel as if I'd been a bit more industrious.

Without a typed-out page, I'm just an amateur. An amateur napper basically. Poetry needs the material world. Even if it's just a stack of paper on my desk. I say, "Type it in. Print it out. Show yourself you made something. Something of yourself." And then you can feel like a happy worker. A happy worker at happy hour. Pay yourself with beers.

I was telling the bartender that I was depending on her stack of cocktail napkins. And I pointed to her apron. At her flat stomach and slim waist and slender hips. And I said, "I'm also depending on that."

"On what?," she asked, looking down at herself.

"On that!" I said again, extending my arm toward her waist and gently reaching into the small pocket on the front of her apron and taking hold of her Bic pen.

Kleenex Boy

When I was in middle school, I had this biological need, as well as compulsion, to constantly wipe my nose. I was nicknamed Kleenex Boy.

I could dig into my pockets at any moment and pull out a seemingly endless inventory of crumpled tissues.

One day, my best friend Ben and I decided to determine exactly how many used tissues were stuffed in my pockets. By the time they were completely emptied out, we'd gotten up to twenty-nine individual tissues—they'd come to be this compacted dense aging sausage in the interior of my khakis.

Some tissues had only been used once, or twice, and had vaguely, if at all, come into contact with my nostrils. While others had been through a bit more wear-and-tear.

Tissues were certainly among the first products designed for instant disposability. I wrote an article for a technology journal out of MIT a number of years ago about a disposable computer that was being designed at the time by Apple for CVS Pharmacy. The concept, at least, was for a squashable computer called the iSheet. Designed to come in a twenty pack and be used only once. Perfect, let's say, to view a single YouTube or fire-off a single e-mail message. It was by then well understood that people enjoy the sensation of throwing things away so much more than turning things on and off. And then there's the joy of holding onto something for longer than its designed longevity.

In the case of my pocketful of tissue paper, I think it actually had more to do with laziness. I was oblivious about hygiene at the time. It was out of pure convenience that I began to use my pants as a trash bag.

As Ben and I examined the collection of snot-rags that had been set out across the big table in the science room, we came to appreciate each specimen's quirky individual character. It was clear to both of us, and the small crowd of classmates that had gathered around, that a few of them possessed more intrigue than others. There was one in particular, that was so deteriorated that it was on the verge of turning back into pulp. I tried to splay it open to examine it more closely and it literally disintegrated in my hands transforming itself into a tiny cloud of air-born lint.

My dad always

complimented me on my swing. Even though I was the strike out king of the entire little league.

I've thought a great deal about his way of comforting me, in praising my disability to connect. Or his reinforcement of my ability to disconnect.

Either way, my fantasy may have been for the batter to find the fastest and most direct route back to the bench. Which is, maybe unconsciously, a matter of only three strikes.

Only once did the perfect swing of my aluminum bat produce a perfect ping. Only once did I hear the high snap of a bell in my ear and gaze out at that ball sailing away in the vast blue sky.

The Bad News Bears may be the most erotic film ever made. Due to the pubescent rebel who revs his dirt bike, pops a wheelie, and guns it across the infield. He's not at home in his room jerking off to a fantasy. No, he's in full penetration of the psyches of those inchoate minds. The tread of his tires marks the actual mud.

My dad

grabbed his keys. And I got in the car with him. We sped off to find the source of the sirens. And when we approached the sharp curve on Caves Road only a few miles away, we saw flashing lights. Our blurry windshield was lit with rosy beads of rain.

My dad rolled down his window and took directions from the firefighter, who waved for him to keep moving. This is when I caught a glimpse of the crinkled cycle jammed up into the guardrail. And the huddle of paramedics way far back in the woods. Working in a rainy ray of light.

Into the

fog. Away from earlier. It was Thanksgiving. The city was so empty. Trains were rolling out in all directions. Like leather belts. Airplanes were packed in a convoy. Along the single lane of sky. Nose to tail. Nose to tail.

The bartender kept topping me off. I asked Brooke if any Greek philosopher had ever spoken about planting seeds in the minds of married women. I insisted to Brooke that she let me pay the bill and that she wait for me out front. I was tired of the rushing street corner. The goodbye. The scene where we embrace. And I feel her hand gently pat my back. Goodnight. As if to say: little boy.

I need a

patient. I've blurted this out in numerous e-mails and at numerous times. I think it's a pretty twisted provocation, to be perfectly honest. An opener, you could say. For skepticism! So much skepticism that I've yet to find anyone to engage me in a discussion on this topic.

I guess this is why I'm talking to myself. In this poem. It's not the call-and-response I wanted, but it'll do.

I was walking toward the Brooklyn Bridge with my intern the other day, pestering her with the absurdity of my need for a patient, and she didn't even give me that giggle I get at work. I guess the giggle is her way of saying, "Stop harassing your intern."

One shouldn't make such a desire known, I guess. Even if one is legitimately a doctor! But it's my off-ness that has potential. Even when I'm slipping. So much so, that I go out of my way to preserve my, let's just call it, perversion.

I suppose doctors shouldn't go around soliciting random healthy people (or healthy interns for that matter). But I'll go first. Future book title: *I'll Go First*.

Maybe I'm sending a warning sign: beware of my other side, my suspicious side, my untrustworthy side. My core is on the warpath. Please know, there's a creative menace in me. Plotting.

I say this to confess that I don't entirely trust myself. And while this can be problematic, I was simply not convinced by my Lacanian analyst to purge my stubborn pride in being awful.

This, I suppose, is my drive. Which I had to have restored. Repaired. This is me. And my own distrust in the product of my creativity means, simply, that I can't fully dominate my wild bucking curiosity.

My patient

stands before a French easel for an hour. In a silent medita-
tive state. Just looking. It is the doctor's job to set the easel in
a location before each session and to notify the patient of
that session's chosen itinerant coordinates. Frame Therapy.

I want to get to the next level, to begin doing actual
hands-on experiments out in the field.

Dilation. I'll keep an inventory of locations, like a location
scout. I'll know them. I'll administer these locations. Based
on a certain, let's call it, mastery of the delirious city. And my
patient, who for now will be known simply as Casey Study,
will appear at each location, session after session. No words
will be uttered between us.

Playing doctor will be my future. Stone sober. Sober as
science. Perhaps I'll even wear a lab coat.

These spelling

errors absolutely must stick. They reflect my computer's
inability to make me conform. To cover up my life-long abil-
ity to think phonetically. To drift in and out of song.

Poetry presented itself to me with my first losing battle to
differentiate "to," "too," and "two." Homonyms were the
only thing in school that I remember learning.

But I have to admit, spell check has always been my friend.
It has saved me from so much embarrassment.

I once thought I could improve my spelling by teaching
myself to write with my right hand. That way, I figured, I'd

80

feel the words slide out under my arm and hang on the paper with the proper letters.

A proper penman I am not. The lefty intuition, born in me, was, and still is, a birth defect. It has crippled me. It has caused me to stay home, collect unemployment, and watch rock videos all day. For a while I was googling anything I could vaguely remember from my youth. Now I've grown bored of everything I can remember.

The last thing that interested me was Queen. At Wembley Stadium in 1985. I noticed that Freddie wasn't like the others. All the other men were trying on femininity. Freddie, on the other hand, was trying on masculinity. Throwing his arm and fist forward! Thrusting out his chin. Smashing his mustache into the testicles of air. In a wife beater. With hairy fucking Gujarat armpits. In tight white jeans. Decathlon-style Adidas.

His microphone was fastened to the upper part of his mic stand. He skipped around with the two-part apparatus as if it were some sort of Shakespearean dagger.

I've never seen anyone copy this.

They've

known all along that it's a small. But they are adamant that I use the word "tall." But why?

My best guess it that they're afraid. But of what? Of small? Yes. They're afraid of small. They're afraid that if I think less of myself, I'll part with less money. And if, on the other hand, I can be influenced (perverted) by language to see myself as a member of the vertically advantaged, I'll then be more inclined to reach. To reach for the absolute limit. The limit of what I'll pay for a simple cup of black coffee.

Up till now, for many many years, I've gotten to the front of the line, kept my head down, and mumbled the word "small." Knowing that my branding lesson is about to begin. And that by the time my hot cup of coffee is handed over to me I'll stand corrected. I'll be that much more brainwashed into seeing myself as a somebody. Not a nobody.

But today something seems to have changed. My spirit seems to have sprouted. I'm no longer resisting being branded. Maybe I've become what they keep telling me I am. A tall. Or at least a little more than a small. I guess I've accepted some aspirational dimension of my psyche. The part of my psyche that pays to play. Perhaps I've accepted agency. Responsibility. My little cog in the wheel. Perhaps I've made, and will live up to, my tall order!

What's really sad about all of this is that there is in fact a third option, that no one knows about. It is, basically a perfect, reasonably priced cup of coffee. It is called the Short. Order a Short, if you dare.

Forty-seven.

Damn, I'm getting up there. As in, over forty. Finally. I'm pleased to say I've crossed the hump of life expectancy. And that I'm finally in decline. Enjoying this breezy downhill glide.

I've been dismissed. Taken off the roster. Of upward immobility. Now I have downward mobility, or gravity, on my side. I'm pretty much nearing free fall. My resistant tight-fisted test has been handed in to the teacher. I'm done with that.

I make

a late entrance. And I'd like to make an early exit so I can finally enter the witness protection program. Let's consider me the last responder. Book title: *The Last Responder to Enter the Witness Protection Program*. I'm just lazy. Ultimately. Title: *Ultimately Lazy*. I'm fundamentally me. Title: *Fundamentally Me*. My problem is that I'm still not sure which poems to read. Tonight. At my reading in Williamsburg. I've been leafing through the stack. Each one is worse than the next. It's a disaster.

I think I'll take a shower. And under the spray of warm water, I realize I'm in such fundamental doubt about… pretty much everything. Rule of thumb: when in doubt, do both.

So I print them all out. All the dictation we've been doing. And go to the reading.

I sit down in the chair with my poems in hand and look out at the bright yet guarded faces of my audience. My grass roots movement. I've been let out of the gate. I have a frozen gunshot in my ear.

seemed mad when he saw Amy in my sweater. He read it as a varsity jacket from the 50s, as in, "she belongs to me."

But this wasn't that at all. It was heavy Chilean wool. And Amy really didn't belong to me, at all. She had sort of helped herself to it off my floor.

The night before, she and Brandon dared me to carve a hole into a canned ham. And sort of, for lack of a better word, fuck it. Right there on the couch. In front of just them.

There was a very ugly photograph taken by Brandon of me doing the dare. With my dick in a sort of wet pink block. Beer cans were strewn everywhere. Along with an empty bottle of Evan Williams. And an ashtray full of crushed cigarette butts.

Amy was also in the picture. In the background. Slightly out of focus, looking very high. She had a cigarette dangling off her lower lip. She was laughing, gorgeously.

A few nights later, Amy called and said that Charley had invited all three of us to go out on his sailboat. He was intending to sail to Hermit's Island, as he called it. It was about six hours off shore.

We picked up munchies and met him at Marina Del Ray at around 11:00 pm. By then, a very thick fog had set in. Charley motored out anyway, despite zero-visibility. Another sailor, who was docked in the marina, shouted over that we should not go out in such treacherous conditions. The guy looked seriously concerned for us.

We got out past the harbor's blinking lights and dense blanket of fog in no time. We were all alone in the Pacific Ocean. Just us. And a sky full of stars and moonlight.

Charley made me second-in-command and stuck me with the wheel, while he and Amy and Brandon went to the bow to smoked a J and jam their hands into a noisy bag of potato chips for what seemed like hours. I heard their laughter, but couldn't leave my post. I was alone.

Eventually, Amy was kind enough to bring the joint back to me as well as the bag of chips.

Then twelve dayglow dolphins covered in phosphorescence swam along with us for at least an hour.

The next thing I knew, I was woken by Charley. He shoved me to the side and took the wheel. He began spinning it with all his might, until we were heading back out to sea away from the shore line, which was less than a hundred feet away.

Charley looked over at me with disappointment. And I think disbelief.

Driving down

the New Jersey Turnpike, somewhere near the outskirts of Baltimore, Yau and I stopped off at our usual rest stop. I think it was called the the Maryland House.

We were on our way to our weekly teaching gig. I was driving and he was riding shotgun. I'd say we resembled Cheech & Chong. Yau being Chong.

Yau was asleep. He was snoring. I guess he'd been up late the night before writing porns, I mean poems.

I parked and we entered Roy's. We grabbed our trays. We inched forward in line. Ever closer to the deep fryer. We got our 3-piece meals, or whatever, and paid the cashier. We took our big waxy paper cups over to the soda fountain.

As dark soda shot into my ice-filled cup, my eyes focused on the work of art hanging on the wall adjacent to the machine. It was Duchamp's *Chocolate Grinder*. I swear to fucking god. It was a goddamn Marcel Duchamp.

Ok, let me break this down. Artworks, as we all know, occasionally get stolen from major museum collections and sold on the black market. But do they wind up hung on the walls of fast-food chains?

Yau and I gobbled down our fried chicken, essentially hosed ourselves off in the men's room, and hobbled with our extended bellies back to the car. We were both buckled up, and I was about to turn the ignition, when I paused. And thought, "I can't let it get away. It has to be mine."

But how was I gonna get it? I had an idea. I told Yau I'd be right back, and I marched right back into Roy's and asked to speak to the manager. They escorted me upstairs to one of the offices and introduced me to a nice gentleman behind a big desk. I handed him my official Maryland Institute College of Art Faculty ID and told him in the lowest octave my balls would allow, that I was going to have to confiscate one of their artworks for "educational purposes." The Roy's manager didn't bat an eyelash. If anything, he dutifully complied. It was as if he were serving his country.

He phoned one of the custodial engineers, and within a few minutes, the Grinder was handed over to me in a black plastic trash bag.

V

We should

start with some dictation. Before I forget what's on my mind. But how can I forget what I don't yet know? Anyway, let's just see what comes out, shall we?

My interest in fast food, as you may not know, goes back to my relatives. My mother's side of the family. I'm more than a little sketchy on all of details. Her grandfather started a diner franchise that in the 50s became one of the first pre-fast food chains. It was called the White Coffee Pot Jr.

Once, when I was young, my mom brought me to their commissary in downtown Baltimore. There was a big black guy in an all-white kitchen uniform working at a gigantic mixer. He was mixing enough batter to make a thousand blueberry muffins.

To this day, when I'm on Amtrak, I go to the bar car, and order a blueberry muffin. And when they heat it up in the microwave, I smell the smell and feel the warmth of that memory.

My distant family eventually gave up the White Coffee Pot Jr. chain and created a second restaurant venture called the Smorgasbord. Like other all-you-can-eat cafeteria-style restaurants around the country, it was ahead of its time in catering to, if not giving rise to, fatsos. While also offering a restful haven for the occasional skinny speedy chain-smoking truck driver.

Every Thanksgiving my uncle would send out an invitation. And our entire extended family would meet at one of the centrally located Smorgasbords. This is where we would gather to eat all we could eat. I remember racing my little brother to the soft ice cream dispenser. It was kind of weird seeing all my cousins in one long line with orange cafeteria trays being served by men and women in hair nets.

At

Yale, they shop for poetry classes. This is in the first few weeks of the semester. They try out teachers. They conduct auditions.

They show up and sit there. With no real curiosity other than to see if you will be funny. If you will make them laugh out loud. So you're like expected to pull one out of your hat. And if you don't, they just walk right out.

A few years ago, I was hired for a semester at Yale. And there was some mix up with the scheduling of my class. And a few days before the start of the semester they had presumably changed the time of my class without informing me.

My morning had started off great. I was right on time. But when I came into the building, Reed shot out of his office and greeted me at the front door with hostility. He asked me where I had been, in a very accusatory tone.

I rummaged through my book bag and found the crinkled paperwork they had sent me only a few weeks prior. I held my fist full of papers in the air.

As the papers clearly showed, I wasn't late. On the contrary. I was an hour early! Motherfuckers!

But what was I going to do? "Close to forty students were packed in the classroom," said my TA, Alexa, who was practically in tears. "I did everything in my power to keep them. For the first fifteen minutes, I pretended that you were about to make a grand entrance. Anything to keep them from ditching. But, one by one, they got up and left the room."

JD was a

typical Whartonite, really. He was trained in economics. He was blind to the bronze Henry Moore installed at the entrance of Steinberg-Dietrich Hall.

JD landed on the corporate ladder right out of college. In finance.

We were reunited the other night over at the Ear Inn, which is when I discovered that, in the fifteen years since the last time I'd seen him, he'd essentially helped build the sub-prime mortgage market and watched it explode and rain down.

But, interestingly, JD couldn't help but brag that he had been the inventor of derivatives. He wanted to take credit for the entire collapse of the banking system.

I gulped. He confessed that a few years before he had managed a floor with over five hundred brokers, and that he'd had to fire them all as the shit began to hit and pile up around the fan. His boss, he said, picked him to do the dirty work, coachable as he was.

JD had acquired a tic. I guess this had come from so many hours in the trenches on the front line of white collar crime. It was a vocal tic. He talked really really fast.

But he still looked great—Rogaine great. Ro-great. I mean the guy has the bald gene. So what's with the full head of hair?

The

Schindler House. I love to think of that house. Barely there, really. On Kings Road. Awaiting the quake.

It began to rain the last time I read in the grassy courtyard. The first few drops landed in unison with my first few words.

Brandon told me it sounded more like a chant. It's true. I was exploring a certain tonal register.

I looked out at the audience in their fold-out chairs set up so nicely on the grassy yard. "How about if we switch places?" I said. And the audience stood up, left their seats and came under the eave. And I walked out and sat in one of the chairs, with my stack of poems, which were quickly becoming spattered with soft drizzle.

Someone kindly handed me an umbrella. It was pure theater.

Her words

somehow carried her being through the iPhone to me. I could see her only when I read her words in type. Text messages and e-mails and poems all work this way. It's amazing really how much personality can squeeze through type. What a great invention: type.

The beach today must be beautiful. I can enjoy it from here. Knowing you are there. While I'm here. In Brooklyn. In the apartment. All by myself.

You're not even there. You're on your way there. You're headed down on the New Jersey Transit. Where you will reconnect with Cole and Hokusai. They are staying there all week, with your parents.

This back and forth seems to work well. It was just last night that I had that beachy sensation. It was when the sun was going down. Day was dozing off. And we were wading into the ocean. Ocean. What a word. It can barely contain itself.

We were passing Cole between us, back and forth, between our arms. I kept commenting: "Isn't it beautiful?" I was elated. Cole only maybe four. I kept expecting everyone around to chime in. Like a chorus.

I kept expecting you to repeat my line. To acknowledge something in the sounding out of the words themselves, which after all, are, as they are spoken, part of the ocean.

I guess my family likes to verbalize beauty. It comes from my dad. He'll pause and take the time to comment. And wait for each of his children to go on the record.

I was with

my daughter Cole at her gymnastics class. There was a lot of excitement that day. Because an actual Olympic medalist was present in the gym. She had come to Elite to do a one-day workshop. Everyone was giddy. Coaches and children alike.

That evening, I tried to explain to Cole that her daddy was also an Olympian. An Olympic Poet. And that he too was a major competitor. And a perfectionist.

And a bronze medalist! And that he too was devoted to challenging moves. To making words do, like, basically, splits, and stuff. And to making words, like, vault.

Cole was looking at me, as if to say: you're trying too hard to make your point. And you're holding me here captive as you try to convince yourself of something that may or may not be true.

Anyway, it was too late to turn back. My next graceful sentence would step, one word at a time, across that narrow balance beam.

Eventually the Olympic Poet will dismount. From life.

Crazy blue

sky. Crazy breeze. The climate! My goodness. I feel like I'm bathing in perfection. The birds are offering gentle reminders.

The moon can hardly wait to get in on the action. My dad, of all people, is plucking out a rendition of *Blue Moon* on his ukulele.

What I read today in Harpers won't compute. My arithmetic must be missing. My subtraction seems not to know a negation so great. The ice in Greenland, the author announced without a hint of equivocation—that a glacier that has been stuck like a cork in a bottle of poison for, like, ever—is rotten. Scientists have stopped having children. They say heat will dry up those of us who don't drown first. Heat will pin us down to extinction by the time my daughter has children. The near future would be forever from now, but plumes of methane are rising from the uncorked ocean floor on this perfect day.

VI

What ever happened to

the idea of Martha's Vineyard? Finding a way to survive there as caretakers in the off-season. What ever happened to the idea of living like two lazy dogs on a sandy carpet soaking up the salty air?

Today I came upon the park bench we sat on when we plotted our first underdog-ish steps. Steps, mind you, that were never taken. Did we ever have a plan? Before we crossed under the big blue shadow and paraded eight blocks down Bedford, and met the guy who started Earwax. I forget his name. But he was cool. He had a single milk crate of albums for sale. That was his store. And there was a Louvin Brothers record playing.

Some day I plan to

cover *Don't You Want Me Baby*. But I want my version to be sung in a baritone. Slowly, like Johnny Cash. Plucked on a bass-y acoustic guitar.

The Human League's hit came on the radio in the campus shuttle bus the other morning, when I was commuting to teach. In and out of reception, I could barely hear it through the bus's horrible speakers. All treble.

I was shivering. My breath clouding the air with each exhalation. Both my hands were shoved like a hand-sandwich in the single ski glove I found earlier that morning.

I see

a concentration camp in my head. Emaciated prisoners made to strip and stand in a line at the edge of a mass grave. Single file, in just their bones. Then the guards open fire. And the humans drop. And "CUT!" I yell through the cone.

I still can't accept this genocide. But why? It must be the embarrassment. Collapsing into a blood-soaked crater with all those other buckled bodies of various age and gender, dead or alive, is not a cool thing. Which is why I can't get this Holocaust down the hatch.

What should I do? Just sit here with my fear and loathing of Treblinka?

I taught a seminar down South last night. I was at VCU in Richmond, Virginia. I took the liberty of engaging my grad students in a conversation about concentration camps. I cracked a beer, took a long swig, and said: "Never beg for your life. Because when you've been blown away, and rolled into a mass grave, at the very least, you will know in your dead head that you died with pride."

And then one of the grad students—a survivor, I think, of a recent genocide somewhere in, like, Hawaii—challenged this presumption. "Of course you should beg for your life." And he elaborated in such a way as to reduce my point to some kind of clichéd, Hollywood heroism. "You sound like you've watched one too many Westerns."

Notice how this student managed to find a way to blame, you know who: the Jews. Hollywood. Anyway, he continued: "Pride can be restored."

But is this true? Can pride be restored? Can a person ever really overcome humiliation? Can a person ever bounce back from bonafide embarrassment? Humans can be revived, brought back from the dead, but can a person's pride ever be restored.

The problem, I say, is not that six million Jews were murdered. It's that six million Jews were embarrassed. The kids laughed from the shock of my comment. I have to say, their laughter felt good.

Maybe there was some way for me to re-envision the genocide. Without so much embarrassment. Without so much humiliation. Maybe I could live with the idea of all the Jews of Europe being gunned down or gassed in broad daylight and bulldozed into a mass grave, if they had just had some clothes on.

So here's my plan: first, I'm gonna audition Christian Bale as my lead. The part will require that he lose sixty pounds. Or more.

He'll play a German Jew who arrives via boxcar in this positively gorgeous rural setting. Consider it the Blue Ridge foothills of Poland.

The Nazis will be like the Penn State football team. There will even be black Nazis with sleeveless uniforms tailored to fit mammoth arms fully etched with ink.

No one in the poem will be even remotely Aryan. A shaggy Keith Moon will be like mulling around with his drumsticks.

In this poem, the Nazi antagonists will not be like the Phillips Academy Andover type that we've grown accustomed to seeing in the movies. They will be diverse Nazis. iNazis. Starbucks Nazis.

At the time of his imprisonment, Christian will have been apprenticing with an old throwback escape artist (picture the Houdini of Berlin). And he will be learning to be a world-class breath-holder.

It is this skill that will allow him to survive the first execution attempt. He'll literally outlast the gas. And when the guards come back in to the showers to scoop up the corpses, he will be hiding behind the door. And make a getaway.

The viewer will come to understand through flashbacks that only a few days prior to arriving at the death camp, Bale had been sitting with his very attractive Aryan-looking girlfriend at a bar talking about Peach Schnapps and Dada. The two hipsters will look something like any two passengers packed shoulder-to-shoulder in the last car of the L Train, circa 2005.

I think I'll ask Sofia Coppola to direct the poem. And I'll reference her dad's score from *Apocalypse Now*. Jim Morrison, mind you, is a perfect example of an anorexic man who may have lost his pride after standing completely naked before the cops.

It's all about apocalypsial coolness. Duval, down on the beach, ordering that soldier to surf the bombed-out waves. Fat and clammy Brando, with his girly lisp. Hopper, with his camera dangling over his shoulders, with spirals in his pupils. Martin Sheen (it goes without saying). And Samuel—who is basically Hendrixian. Who else? The cool gay dude with the puppy. (Wait, I think he was the surfer). Essentially, anyone American is cool. In a sort of Hunter S. Thompson, mirrored-Ray-Ban-ish way.

Bale will be thrilled to take part in this story. He'll be psyched to let his emaciated body do its thing. Thrilled to let his scrotum hang in the wide open gap between his hollow groin, as some pervert coach barks in his ear.

The poem will be made for whatever budget. And that's it. Easy as pie. Easy as an episode of *Hogan's Heroes*. Easier!

Here is how I envision the ending: Bale will line up for the firing squad and prepare to finally die. He will get his heart rate way down, and enter into a deep hallucination. He'll hold his breath, and keep holding. It will be his last breath. He will be relaxed. He won't beg for survival. He'll have a touch of evil in his eyes. He'll arch back and flop onto the dirt mattress. His ball sack will swing like a ripe bell. His lungs will turn to steel. And the poem will end. Before the bullet has ever been fired.

Only then will we ponder this bullet. And travel with it. In slow motion. Through zero humidity. Off into the silky grass. Off into the sun-kissing trees—trees that will never whisper another word about any of this.

I taught

a stand-up comedy class. I wanted to bait the administration into firing me. Into putting me out of my adjunct misery. In a way, it had become like *The Isle of Dr. Moreau* down there in Baltimore.

I felt a bit like Brando, with a family of furry cyborgs, all somewhat of my own creation. I could feel the point of mutiny drawing near. Even the most loyal of my students were beginning to question my validity. And my sobriety!

Maybe I was trying to do the impossible. Trying to get *them* to do the impossible—to transform their traumas into well-crafted units of verbal self-deprecation.

I seemed, at that point in time, at least, to know how this could be done. And on the night of the stand-up comedy show, it felt like my night.

As the off-campus loft began to fill up with students, and more students, and even *more* students, my kids began to get increasingly, almost debilitatingly nervous. I called them into a huddle backstage. Never before have I seen such terror in the eyes of my students. One kid actually begged not to perform. And I granted her this wish.

Over the next forty minutes, they began to break down, one by one. There were sobs. There were disappearances. They were like shivering soldiers in an invading U boat pissing their pants and vomiting.

Before long, the first kid was out on stage. It was too late to turn back. He was met with almost immediate laughter. And within a few seconds his confidence kicked in. He totally forgot about the rest of us. He forgot that there was life off stage. He went well past his allotted 15 minutes. I couldn't get his attention. I couldn't get him off the stage! I was giving him that signal pretending to run a knife across my neck! He ignored me! He was having too much fun! He never wanted it to end! He had no intention of ever coming down!

Ever!

At the end of the magical night, after all the kids had performed, after they had all been dipped into the bath of laughter, there was only one thing left to do. Hug.

It was like the end of SNL when the comics all crowd the stage. And the cameras pan back. And the credits roll. And the tweaky alto plays.

Maybe you should

write this down. Or no, maybe not. Um, yes, please, do. Do! Write this down!

It's early. But I'm gonna uncork this bottle. And thanks for bringing the rotisserie chicken. Remind me to reimburse you. Ok?

So let me just start by saying, I have some rules around here. And if I abide by them, I get to live the unorthodox life. With the unorthodox wife. Which is why I keep the place so tidy.

But I do cut corners. Instead of pushing the vacuum back and forth, I get down on my knees and crawl around, searching for particles. I stare closely. And get out my tweezers. And I tweeze every particle I see. One by one. Every fuzz. Every crumb. From every crust. Of every bread. Because I dread being tangled alive in that horrific extension cord.

I remember bliss. In childhood. When Bessie would vacuum from room to room. The entire suburb would fall into a peaceful hum. It was like a serial raga (see La Monte Young).

Bessie was also the inventor of one of the most uplifting scents I have ever had the great fortune of breathing in through my nostrils. I still use Bessie's formula. Religiously. One top of Pinesol into a bucket of hot water. Followed by a drop or two of Murphy's Oil Soap. And then one other ingredient.

There's a

YouTube. In it an art conservator works in a fluorescent cave. He demonstrates exactly how Ad Reinhardt concocted his extremely evocative black paint.

He squeezes a tube of Mars into a coffee can, and then fills the can with pure mineral spirits. He then covers the can, shakes it up, and puts it down on the shelf, where it is left to sit overnight.

The conservator returns the next morning to his underground cave, and pours the inky liquid through a cotton rag, leaving behind an oily muck, which he quickly discards.

The conservator then dips his flat brush into the can of filtered paint, and slides the brush across the surface of a small canvas positioned faceup on the table. Then comes a second stroke. And a third.

A few hours later the camera returns to that small black canvas demonstrating how the paint dried. Perfectly matte. And without a single brush mark.

It's hard to forget

and even harder to believe how my college professor died. She was on her way to her half-built cabin in Maine, when she was attacked by asthma. She dropped on a snow bank near the car on a lonely highway.

I went to bat for Susan once. Gave her lawyers my deposition when they came on to help her sue the University of Pennsylvania for something involving gender discrimination.

Susan didn't take such good care of herself. Her inhaler was always running on empty. Once when she was wheezing pretty heavily, I reach into my pocket and offered her a puff of mine.

We were standing outside the painting studio chatting about Fairfield Porter, when I noticed how beautiful her eyeglasses were. They were hanging from a black string around her neck. They were in a Chinese style. Maybe vintage.

About a year later, when I discovered that I had astigmatism and needed glasses, I went out and bought her exact same dark frames. And I also attached them to a black string.

I wanted to let my glasses dangle around my neck. Like a real painter.

From now on

Jon Schueler will be referred to as my godfather.

And the Maryland corn fields in late July with stalks blocking distant hills that hold a golden stain of sky, will be my place of origin.

Douglas Dunn was describing something when he flung his hand in front of me. Inches from my ear. Just outside the portal I was peeking through at the time. His hand was like an arrow shot from a bow.

Dance! A blurt of motion. The heart's runny plums. I told him poetry is a sport. The good sport of losing. And the poet is the good sport. The good sport who plays to lose. But to lose elegantly.

I slid

my hand down Eva's back, under her pants, and under her panties, giving her tush a soft squeeze. That was goodbye. She no longer lets me try to kiss her goodnight, so what else can I do? Hug her?

I told her I was considering suing Penn. For failing to provide me with an education. The only class I even liked was taught by a German. In German! And I don't even speak a word of German. Really. Wasn't it someone's job to steer me a little.

Now I'm a teacher and I steer my students plenty. I try to get them anywhere near the road.

I teach drama. I drag them by the hair around the room. I

scream in their faces. I call them "Lazy!" I ask them to take out their ear buds.

The other day I told a student to sit down and give some thought to my advice. I said, "Make a construction site in your mind. Block off the entire region with yellow caution tape. And put out a sign saying ARTIST AT WORK."

"Or," I asked, "would you prefer to lower the bar until the bar is literally on the ground? Is your goal in life to just step over *that* bar? As if you have performed some kind of magic trick?"

But who am I to speak? I have a voice in my head asking me please see the writing on the wall. "Sueleen," the black man's voice pleads, "you may as well face the fact, you cannot sing! You ain't never gonna be no star! I mean, I wish you'd give it up now! I mean, they're gonna kill you! They're gonna tear your heart out if you keep going! They're gonna walk on your soul girl!"

I was walking

Ponyo, when I came upon a sparkling new Lexus parked out in front of my brownstone. It was idling. But with no driver in sight. I stood there for a few minutes listening to its monotonal groove, expecting the car's driver to dash out of one of the nearby buildings, hop in the car, and drive away. Who leaves their unmanned car running for that long? A few more minutes and still no driver. Ponyo, beside me, alert, patient on her leash.

I crept up to the tinted window and peeked in. I reached out and grabbed the door handle. It opened. I quickly shut it.

I looked around. Thoughts were racing through my head. I could steal this car. I could drive it to Pt. Pleasant Beach. And hawk it for a jet ski or something. Or a dozen raw clams on the half shell.

The next morning, when I swung open my front door, there it was. The Lexus! It was still idling in park. All night on one tank of gas.

My left

hand was in a cast. Healing after a hard shot from close range crushed a small bone in the top knuckle of my pinky finger. Cory was across the continent kayaking with dolphins when it happened.

Around that time, I remember driving home with my mom from DC. We'd gone to see the Francis Bacon retrospective at the Hirshhorn. This is when I decided to quit sports. The same way I had quit other things.

And about two decades later, when the word *quitter* came up in therapy, what did I do? I quit therapy.

Had Bacon caused this inner revolt? As I see it, two bodies were in me wrestling, competing, to win my future.

But as it turns out, quitting didn't let me off the hook. The poet's objective is the same as the goalie's: to stand one's ground. To react.

To, by reflex, step in front of high-speed time. To keep life from whizzing past untouched. To remain with my goal, relaxed yet pounded by heart. A projectile among projectiles.

I live with post-traumatic stress disorder. Your basic nervous wreck. Like a war vet. After constant point-blank, point-blank, point-blank. My hand still aches when clouds roll over and play dead. My eyes still quiver when I catch something in the corner.

I'm still called on by my past to perform my honorable duty. To be my last line of defense. Even when there's nothing to defend. Even when competition is nowhere in sight. When the game has gone tranquil. When there's nothing but a bird chirping, the sound of a power saw cutting wood off in the distance, and that of a jetliner even further.

I only

just fiddle around on this rickety old snare. And badly beaten floor tom. And usually I just peter out midsong.

And yet, band practice is still the high point of my day. Fulmer uses his Floridian drawl to cast a spell on Hokusai. She lays at my feet, and rests her head on the rubber shell of my sneaker. And she lets her head bob up and down every time I stamp my foot on the high-hat's peddle.

I've been playing sonic lullabies. Strumming my open-tuned guitar (the black Strat Mini I bought for Cole that has the black Chucks sticker on the pick guard) for about an hour at a whisper on a fuzzy amp until Cole is asleep. Windy chords.

I feel like my nerves are frayed. Or like I'm experiencing some kind of inner mist…hoodie! Hoodie! Now that's a good band name. That's worth going in front of the public for.

Where did I go wrong? Why didn't I get a good teaching job? Was it the rumors? I should have worn my headdress to the interview. If Jews are now the presidents of all the Ivy League universities, certainly they can hire at least one Native American to teach a few rituals to freshman art students.

I guess I'm like Lenny Bruce. He had to go out and do stand-up in order to teach the children.

I have a bit of depression in my fingernails. It came with re-entry. After I returned from Marfa. When I was no longer drinking that water. With the mellowing effect of its high lithium content.

Marfa was like Mayberry. Why can't I be Otis? Mayberry's town drunk. He who has the key to the only jail cell. He who has special permission from Andy and Barney (Don Knots) to crash there while sleeping one off.

Hangover. Another good band name!

I was at the

pool on a crowded Saturday. There were like three other people already in the lane. And I got in. And I quickly realized that this woman was dominating the lane, making it pretty much impossible for anyone else to pass. She even had the gall to use a kickboard. I was stuck behind her white water of fluttering bubbles, loathing her more and more with each lap.

And when I finally had an opportunity to pass her, she veered over to, like, I want to say, block me.

So what did I do? I stood up. And I made her stop. And I got goggle-to-goggle with her. And I let her have it: "Have you ever heard of lane etiquette?" I asked, which is when I uncontrollably waved my arm through the air, and gave the woman a very slight smack on the side of her head, as if to say "Wake up!" The problem was that this gesture made a shockingly audible splat on her tight swimming cap. And it was a move that certainly could have been considered assault. A move that was now too late to remove.

I was too embarrassed to apologize, so I pushed off into another lap. Down and back I had gone when I saw three burly lifeguards standing at the pool's edge waving for me to get out of the water and come with them.

By now the woman was in the safety of the guard office screaming hysterically in what was an Israeli or Russian accent. I was escorted into the lifeguard office and given a chance to tell my side of the story. About five of the other guards were standing around in their red trunks quietly observing. And another guard came in and handed the woman an ice bag.

I don't know. I still don't think it's right to hit a woman. Or a man. Had it been Heath Ledger, I don't think I would have smacked him. I'm referring to when Heath swam the butterfly that day hogging the lane. And I got out of the pool and kicked one of his Adidas sandals right out into the lane, as if to say, "Chew this Mr. Six Pack!"

And he stood up, mid-lap, and started calling me into the water. Not that I knew at the time that it was Heath Ledger. I didn't learn this until way later.

A few months later, Cory and I rented *Brokeback Mountain*. I was enjoying the movie very much when Cory paused it and told me that the actor we were watching lived near us. And swam at our Y.

VII

Hard to say

what has me. With howling wind. In my head. Holding the bed covers over.

My cave. Not a soul knows I'm here. And yet, I'm really out, you know. Not in. Out. Out on the stage. In the spot light. In the spot. In the sparkle of articulation.

I'm a party animal. Across from you.

Some of us seem to be speeding up. But what about me? Older now, I'm with my ego. We're too fat to move.

Sun coming up. Skim-coating the chalkboard morning. It's rise and shine. Hard though. To keep shining. From within. Like leather shoes. Good title: *My Heart is a Pair of Black Dress Shoes in Need of a Shine*.

Chocolate bars are my eyes in a fuzzy shell. It's okay. My eyes reflect off my nose.

It's starting to rain. People on the street begin to hustle. A young woman stops me to ask for directions. And I point her in the right direction. I hold out my umbrella until she takes it in her hand. And I continue on my way.

Follow

me. I'm over here. I wave my arm. Without looking back. Believing, I suppose, that all of human history is behind me. All of human history standing with me. And now I'm old, I guess. Prematurely ancient. I peek back over my shoulder. And what do I see? Nada. Not a thing. Not even a smiling dog whipping its tail. Not even my family. They fend for themselves. And they know I don't even know what money is. My head is a head of iceberg lettuce. Browning. I'm unknown now more than when I started this square dance. Still without a population of alternating partners to swing and be swung by. Alternating partners to cling to and be clung by. I'm pretty far adrift. And yet… (whisper) and yet—I've always been claimed. Overly shopped. Never left to rot.

Words

return to me, as if I were we. You and me. Who is this thing I call "you?" They—the words—fall. On deaf ears. And the drill is done.

An illusion of communication. Will these words ever be utilized? Accessed?

Do I hide in my silt? Do I dread the day I'm dredged up? Or will I wash up? When I've finally given up?

This is a waste. A waste of my one taste of the salty broth of time.

And yet… (*sotto voce*) and yet—I procrastinate! I usually don't even write the poem. These words are usually left in the lottery of my brain. My hit record gets left revolving; no one ever reaches over to gently set down the needle.

My life is like the word that isn't a word. Even after I check its definition.

But I feel I'm speaking with traction. Like sandpaper across pine. I'm gouging valleys in the silver earth. This poem is a propeller. A motor that turns over as I type. It runs infinitely. The poem was left on all night. And all day. What a waste. A light left on in a vacant room.

It will exhaust the minor miracle of its glow off the cloudy walls that extend the shadow of a nerve. Round-the-clock flairs, shot from a life raft. Personalities breezing through and shaking the water into a chop.

Maybe I'm an honest man in need of an alibi. Someone to see me fall in the forest. Someone to vouch for the crime of my wasted time.

I shot

another macro close-up today of a fucking cheeseburger. The burger was printed on a poster in the window of Micky D's. My picture was actually a picture of another macro picture that had already been taken of a well-styled burger. A studio shot.

The American cheese was especially striking. The American cheese that defines, well, everything! In this life, at least.

We know it will melt. In our global microwave. We know the cheese will soon melt.

I'd like to add gold glitter to the mold, and forge it myself. I'd like for the cheese to sparkle. I'd like to craft the new Kraft single.

In American Apparel

I feel old. Especially when I ask one of the hotties for help. Does she adore me? Am I her hang up? I ask myself, as she hangs up a rainbow row of hoodies.

It would take five minutes to gut the entire store and turn it into a CVS. How many pharmacies will there be before we all get stuck out here alive? For eternity? Now we have a pharmacy on every corner. And all the drugs are sold over-the-counter.

Anyway, I was there at American Apparel to make a return. A grape-colored hoodie. I'm trying to convert this hoodie back into money. I'm trying to accumulate coins from the proverbial "sofa crack."

It's return season. For me. My poverty has finally become, well, apparent. American Apparent. That should be the store's name. I've arrived here at the end of unemployment.

Yesterday, I sold a few art books on my stoop. I was sitting out there all day like a store owner. I threw in one of my daughter's *My Little Pony*'s with that Hanna Darboven biography. I made pretty good money. But I decided to donate all of my earnings to the bartender.

"I'd like a full refund," I said to the kids playing in their parent's store. The young lady with lots of eye make-up on eyed the protrusion stretching out the pocket of my gray hoodie. "I know that's not a gun. It's your finger," she said.

"All my tees are torn," I told her. "Each tear starts as a hole at the corner of the pocket and grows and grows." I ripped off my hoodie so that she'd see my hole-y T-shirt.

I break a sweat now simply doing the dishes. I'm *that* out of shape. A patch of drops first appears across the clingy chest region. A damp shadow then forms running all the way down the middle of my back.

I now pack a second tee when I go out to the bar. This way, I'll have a dry one to change into.

I looked

across the Polaski Bridge. As I sipped black coffee through a crack in a white plastic lid. We've all done this.

I actually tried to play my guitar today. I tried to sound like Joe Pass. Haha. If you know Joe Pass, you know how NOT like Joe Pass I would have sounded.

The neck of my 1963 Gibson is still covered with blue masking tape. It was never meant as anything more than a temporary splint.

I'm yet to get sad about David Weinstock's suicide. But that's how this cocktail works. My "meds," so to speak. Keepin' me cool. Or maybe I just don't care about Dave's death. And maybe he doesn't care about the eventuality of mine?

Before I put Hokusai down, I saw my reflection one last time in her milky brown eyes. I squeezed my nose to her pasty dehydrated muzzle.

Jim

keeps inviting me over. Why? Why is he trying so hard to get me out of my house? And into his? Why not meet in neutral territory? Say at a bar? Where there might be an ostensible honey bee?

I'd rather not talk about Robert Creeley again with a bunch of male poets at a long kitchen table laden with sections of an over-read Sunday Times and like six different hot sauce varieties.

I'd like to be challenged by something! By someone! Charmed. Or maybe seen as charming. To get a female to smile. To have her leave with a planted seed in the forest behind her eyes. Giggle is the first step towards wiggle.

A *challenge*. This is the word I use. Which proves, in a certain way, that I am not a new-comer to rejection. But it's hard to speak about desire these days. I think I said, "Women are beautiful when only their eyes can be seen." And everyone at the table attacked me for being a misogynist. I guess one is not supposed to paint a portrait of a woman entirely veiled by a burqa? God forbid I had commented on the sex appeal of an 18-year-old Hassidic woman in Baltimore's best lycra Under Armour attire with two children in the kiddy pool.

What am I doing here? This event is all writers. And nobody seems to recognize me. Even though I'm the only Peter Falk in the room. A character among authors. They look like one big happy clan of unrelated Ikea-shoppers. They all look like caricatures rendered in the New Yorker of coming-of-age first-book-award winners. Are fiction writers sexy? Only if you like men who look like dads.

I was

a bully. Frankly. And I bullied a guy named Larry. I stuffed him into this canvas laundry cart (they're actually called "basket trucks") and rolled him up and down the hallway. Perhaps mortified, he cried. This is how the fucking short story about the bully ends.

But the poem goes on. About my diet. That I broke last night. With multiple pulled-pork sliders.

And about the way I tidy up now every day. I make the bed. Around three. After I get up. I'm quite proud of this. I'm proud of my bed-making ability. Whoever reads my eulogy, I'd like to request that you say: "He made a good bed."

Right now I'm under the covers. It's a cool noon in autumn. The city sounds like an internal combustion engine. Out the window. A tall tree throws an office party. A short tree moves not an inch. I'm lead in a cheer by a sky with its white pom-poms held high.

Naps are underrated. Horizontality is logical. So is whispering. I address my dog in a whisper. You try. Ponyo. Shhhhhh. Ponyo. Again. This time even quieter. Call her in a whisper. Shhhhhh. She will hear you. She will come.

I want to be

watched so bad. I want a voyeur to be here so bad. A secret admirer.

Snowden just doesn't get it. He doesn't realize that we all want it. We all want to be watched. We all want to be watched so bad.

We're all so bad. We think we're so good. "I've got nothing to hide," we say.

Edward should have asked me first. He should have asked permission. Or for a second opinion. What does Jer want? What do we all want? A few of us seem to want privacy. But not *all* of us. Some of us want to be spied on.

By whoever will take pains to watch and listen. CIA, FBI, whoever. By whichever government agency is willing to give us the time of day.

I enjoyed shopping at the Middle Eastern grocery. On Atlantic Ave. I just couldn't get myself to go that extra half-block. To Traders. I'm so sick of Trader Joe's. They aren't trading squat.

I brought in three used poetry books and a Walter De Maria monograph. They wouldn't accept any of these quality items for barter.

I got a falafel. And I ate it, standing on the sidewalk. It was so delicious that I went back into the Middle Eastern grocery and asked them to sell me every product in the falafel they had just served me. I wound up putting 75 dollars of stuff on my debit card. The next day I made my own falafel, and you know what? It was horrible.

I'm Jeremy Reynolds now. My British accent lessons are going well. And today I was very industrious. I sat down and taught myself three bossa nova chords.

On my walk, I encountered two Chinese teenagers fishing at Pier Five. The day was, well: on its gorgeous way. Not a cloud in the hamper of sky. The two boys were reeling one in. There was so much drama. Their cigarettes burning faster and faster with each inhalation. No hands to flick the ashes.

They unhooked their big fish. And I stopped to, well, congratulate them (catching a fish is a big fucking deal where I come from). And here's where I did something very weird and maybe somewhat out of character. I walked right up and gave one of the guys a pat on the back. And I signaled to the other guy that I wanted to give him a high-five.

He left me hanging. Probably thinking, in Mandarin: what's with this douche?

In one high school play

I played a post office clerk. A dimwit. The director coached me to act totally isolated from everybody. And everything. I was to remain buried in my Walkman. And to sporadically haul an overstuffed mail sack across the stage. And push my basket truck filled with letters and other parcels from place to place.

I have an interesting theory: the high school plays we act in foreshadow our futures. I did, for instance, grow up to sort mail into alphabetical slots in a lonely post office. And I did grow up to be just like the romantic poet I played in George Bernard Shaw's *Candida* (Marchbanks). And Mike Pursley did die. Only a year after his character died in the O'Neill play, *Long Day's Journey into Night*.

My role as the dimwit, anyway, was to provide sadness. As well as comic relief. At one point, the director had me stop in my tracks, let my heavy mail sack down, approach one of my female co-workers, and ask her out on a date. A retard and an old lady painting the town red. Not even Casavettes would have been so audacious. It was in the league of *Titicut Follies*.

The boring office-working woman, anyway, was played by none other than Ceres Horn. Her character was apparently a year away from retiring. SHIT! Now I remember! My God! The play was set in a government office! We were the Internal Revenue Service! We were the IRS!!! We were collecting taxes for God's sake! Jesus! What kind of high school play is that???

I did, however, as a result of the play, get to know Ceres Horn fairly well. It was one year before she graduated early from high school and waddled off to Princeton's astrophysics department. Ceres did actually waddle. And she did actually wear eye glasses with seriously thick coke-bottle lenses. Nothing about Ceres didn't in some way contribute to her uncanniness.

She and I had this moment together. We bonded. We were backstage during the intermission. I was complaining of a headache, when she instructed me to sit in front of her, facing away. She scooted up behind me. I closed my eyes as she applied even pressure to my temples. She concentrated and, I guess, entered my mind, telepathically.

Here's the shocker: Ceres died the following year in a horrible Amtrak derailment. And with her in my mind, fused to my temples, I can still feel the sadness. Google it if you want to check the facts.

I think

I'd rather die on an Amtrak, in a way, than live forever on one, commuting on the toilet seat.

I'd stay in the locked little bathroom all the way down to Baltimore to avoid being spotted by the conductor and made to show the ticket that I didn't actually have. Down and back, week after week. Between the two Penn Stations, which were about three hours apart.

I had so many trips with that one mousey conductor. He'd pick on me. Not because I looked poor. But because I looked like I didn't have to work no more.

The last art opening I attended in Chelsea, I was told by this sexy gallery director (who was, like, a widow, and quite good at flirting for commissions) that in my slovenly, somewhat weathered unshaven appearance, I looked like I'd just docked my yacht at Chelsea Piers and come ashore to purchase a work of art for my summer house in Maine. My look seemed to say: early retirement.

VIII

When I got

bored of YouTubing Eagles and Chicago hits, I switched over to Eagles and Chicago NFL films. A subconscious link. The slow motion reels were put to militaristic narration and dramatic symphonies. In one segment, a defenseman tried to bring down a running back. He clung with one hand to the ballcarrier's mesh jersey. And the highly elastic shirt stretched and stretched, and finally gave way. The runner literally bursted right out of his own shirt! He then took a few more strides into the end zone and spiked the ball, with his naked shoulder pads flipping and flopping in the cold air. Today such a spectacle would be considered a wardrobe malfunction.

I'm reminded of puberty, when I decided to shred my underwear one day. To transform the elastic white briefs into something Tarzan-ish. And to stand in front of the bathroom mirror until the thrill wore off.

I got

robbed. But I also robbed. Actually I got caught red-handed. While attempting to rob the walk-in refrigerator behind the Fox & the Hound. Red-handed. With a six pack of St. Pauli Girl.

I was chased across the parking lot by the entire staff of waiters and bartenders in their forest green aprons and crimson polo shirts.

The cops eventually came. A lawyer was hired. A deal was struck. I got off working three long nights as their cheerful dishwasher.

They were overly-forgiving. By the end of my time, they had somewhat sided with the criminal. It was with distinct pleasure that they led me out to the walk-in refrigerator and pointed to the brand new security camera that had just been installed.

I yelled

at the principal of the Catholic girls school. From the edge of the stage. I went berserk in front of the packed gymnasium. I yelled my lungs out at the stuffy official. Apparently she didn't like our noisy rock-n-roll band, and decided to send one of her students on a mission backstage. The little girl crept around back there until she found the orange heavy-duty extension chord that led to the power strip that led to our amplifiers and PA system. And she pulled it out of the socket! We were midway through our cover of the Clash's

Should I Stay or Should I Go when the small red light on my amp went dark.

The reason

I do not make paintings, I now realize, is a good one. It is to avoid redundancy. Allow me to explain: Jon already made the paintings I would make. He painted them. When I saw them for the first time, in a way, they swam right up through my eyes like sperm. And they impregnated me.

They colored my heart. I followed their inspiration. But out they would not come.

So I had no choice but to covet them, keep them in. Internalize them. Let them inhabit. Let them haunt me.

While Jon has been dead for some time now, his spirit is still riding in me. His spirit wants to see how much further it can go. Now I am the medium. I am the paint and paint brush.

Perhaps I was born NOT to paint, but to use restraint. I still face Jon's blank canvas. Standing next to Jon's palette. Slathering Jon's wide house-painting brush. Causing paint to spring from its bristles and flex across the soft expanse. I still feel my shoulder rotating and going with the nerves that flow down to my hand, till paint hovers like a cloud misting off the wind.

And other clouds drift. And shift. Into and out of place. Pale lavender melting into a lemony gray before slipping away. Crossing, it obscures an earlier rash of peachy violet.

I can feel a frizzy feeling in my gut. Forks of lightning seeking the ground. The painting interlocks in a sort of quivering field of undulation.

This sky is what Jon referred to as his *search*. Initially, it was a search for his mother, who died giving birth to him. But then it became a search to rediscover the shadow-speckled land he had viewed through the glass womb of his B-17 bomber.

We moved on

to a juicier question: what artist should hang in the bedroom? Pierre Klossowski. I see it over our Harvey Ellis chest of drawers.

Do you remember what we did to get that chest? Do you remember how much we cared? About a dumb old piece of furniture.

I'd say I was in the grips of a Gustav Stickley obsession. Right before or was it after my Carl Andre obsession. Which was right before or after my woodsy Neil Welliver obsession.

I remember Paul McCarthy taking notes in a little spiral pad during my lecture on Neil. He asked, "Neil who?" and I spelled out the name W-E-L-L-I-V-E-R. Look him up.

Cory and I were nesting, I guess. It was just before we bought the beach house and installed the—you guessed it—wood-burning stove. Just in time for our first Pt. Pleasant winter. A cord of firewood was delivered that simply would not burn right. Each log would only smolder. For hours. No matter how hot the oven.

We stood there, anyway, in front of the chest at the furniture store trying to get up our nerve to sign the check. The saleswoman pulled out the bottom drawer and stepped in, to prove how strong it was. And, I think, to show how nice her legs were. I'm glad we bought it. Even if it's petite drawers are hardly big enough to hold like a single pair of socks.

When I bought these socks, the girl behind the register told me that she knew me. "I'm Chelsea White," she said. "I took a class with you when I was in art school. And I actually came out in your class!"

I smiled. But I was hit with this unfortunate pang of anger, this regretful little voice in my head asking: "Shouldn't she give me the socks? As a small token of her appreciation?" Oh well. I leaned in, raised my hand, and gave her a high-five. There was something glorious about our arching clapping palms over the cash register and the rack of lip gloss. And the colorful scrunchies.

What is that

hanging over the side of the bun? I'll tell you what it is. It's an orange slice of cheese. It grips the ledge of the burger. But it certainly is not one with the burger. It is its own thing. An autonomous structure. I can imagine it so much bigger. Oldenbigger. Like Oldenburg-er.

I'd like to scale it up and create a monumental, wrestling-mat-sized Kraft Single. You know? Foam dipped in some kind of orange rubber. I'd like to feel it pucker. Under the weight of my wrestling shoes (and in my wrestling singlet).

Did I tell you yet about my idea to substitute the orange dye with black dye? I mean, like, why should American cheese be orange? I want American cheese to be black. Matte black. To look like black leather. Imagine a hamburger in a black leather jacket.

Yesterday was somber and somehow a held breath of the day-by-day inhalation-exhalation of it all. I'm reminded of poor Hitoshi. Who fell from a ladder to his premature death.

Yesterday I spent most of the morning surfing YouTubes from September 10th, 2001. I kept trying to substantiate the thunderclap I swear I heard that afternoon. The day before 9/11. This single thunderclap shook the house around 3:00 pm. With enough power to make me stop and wonder why the building hadn't caved in.

But I never was able to find any report of thunder or even stormy weather in Brooklyn on that day—the day before Dick and Don put their plan into action. (P.S. It turns out that Hurricane Erin was hovering off the coast of Long Island on 9/10 and 9/11).

He

came into my room and lumbered over to a messy table, where he started flipping through my scattered collection of CDs. He then mumbled something about having never listened to music before. Hilarious. And he picked up a Ray Charles disk and began to examine it. "Hey look," he said, with a dumbfounded, spaced-out, stoner expression, "this guy has the same name as me. But backwards."

Charley would often employ me to do small jobs on his sailboat. I would ride shotgun in his dark green Toyota pickup fearing for my life as he raced like a bat out of hell up the coastal highway towards a marina in Oxnard.

I actually learned something about sculpture as I observed Charley's approach to "the art of sailboat maintenance." If he needed to screw something in, we'd get in the truck, drive all the way to the hardware store, and buy, like, one screw.

By the time we'd get back to the boat with our one screw, he'd realize we didn't have a screwdriver! So we'd drive back to the hardware store and buy a screwdriver.

Finally he'd complete the simple task. And then, while cleaning up, Charley would toss out the screwdriver.

Not to brag

but they were sort of in awe of me. Which is not to say that they liked me. They sort of hated me. Why? Because I had sort of destroyed them. One class at a time.

Each week we'd walk to the edge and, "Okay, hit the deck! Grab on tight! Stretch your necks! Peek out over the cliff! Reassemble your eyes on that tiny world!"

One student was a pretty mature woman—who initially felt harassed by me (sort of) and kept pushing back at me (sort of). But she was no longer resistant. She was now just quietly observing my outside-facing-in-facing-out. Who knows? I had a hard laugh with Gina at the bar the other night when I told her that I had somehow wound up with a

139

bitter old lady in my sophomore seminar and that the woman wouldn't stop heckling me.

Anyway, I must have pounded her into submission. But not with cruelty. Just by making her aware how cruel it—Art—can be. Every week, I'd introduce my class to a new outsider—a new dysfunctional, addicted, well…dick. In the long history of dicks. I included women too. Female dicks.

I even showed a clip from the new movie starring Robert Redford, *All is Lost*. Why? Because I wanted them to see that remarkable patch-job he did on the gaping hole in the hull of his yacht—which may be the greatest work of assemblage I've ever laid eyes on. Far better than any piece by Schwitters or Rauschenberg.

All the adventure in detail of the lonely fact of my "take" on things. And my take-it-to-the-hoop of things. Week after week. That's all it was.

Eventually the last class of the semester rolled around, and I was poised to give my goodbye speech. And on the train ride from Brooklyn I entered through the automatic sliding doors of my brain and pushed a cart down the parallel aisles looking for a few last ingredients…a few last words of wisdom to include in the survival kit I was giving them. That's what it was. That's what I had been preparing for them all semester. A survival kit.

Backtrack to the first class. I swear I came at them like an entire Special Team on a kickoff. Here's what I said: "Don't rush me. Ok? Really. Don't fucking rush me! I don't want to feel inhibited by your collective anxiety. What are you so anxious about anyway? I know the answer. You're afraid I'm gonna lose my train of thought. You're afraid I'm gonna forget my lines." I smiled and walked over to the heckler: "You're afraid I'm gonna forget what I'm saying, aren't you?"

She smiled.

And YOU TOO! reading this. Relax. I'll get there. OK? Don't rush the poet.

And then I changed the topic to the word "curiosity." Ah, the lost art of curiosity. Or How to Surf the Internet. I talked about the apparent "atrophy of play," and told them how I had once mastered the "clicker" while watching MTV with my brother back in the 80s.

So here I was, ready to level out and land this Airbus, with the naked awkward aging quality of my hard nose and graying armpits. "What three words," I asked, "meant the most all semester?" No one moved. No one even blinked. No one dared raise a hand. "Three words. Ready?"

"Curiosity?"

"Yes. Curiosity. The first is curiosity. No doubt you'll need that."

"Reflection?"

"Indeed. Reflection. The second word is reflection. Nobody understands the importance of reflection—of reflecting, that is, on what one has done. And what one is about to do. Don't prepare. Be unprepared. But reflect! So that when you are ready to act you will do so with spontaneity. And accuracy. So that you will reach through the tube sock of time and speak the little muppet of your mind. OK? Got it? Good. So now here's the third word for your survival kit. It's the last word I want to say to you."

141

I stopped. The biggest challenge, I now realized, would be letting something out while simultaneously holding something in. Only part of it—the word—could be safely expressed. Too much emotion was clinging to whatever word was cocked and loaded and about to manifest. "And the third word is…optimize. Optimize the experiment. Recognize its excess and irrelevance and redundancy and distraction. Take the optimal step—take the best step you can. Take the step of optimal un-knowing."

I took out my phone and googled the word, and scrolled down numerous Wikipedia definitions. I tipped my glasses off my forehead onto the bridge of my nose. Like a welder. Now the room was frozen. Waiting. No one was rushing me. "Be opti…be opti…be…" And a shiver shot from my toes up my spine into my sinuses. And my eyelids flung open like velvet capes. I was now on the ledge looking out through a glaze. And I grabbed my composure, blinked three times, and said: "Be optimistic. I guess." I nailed it—my dismount. Like in the Olympics. And I held my gaze to the highest point in the room, tilting up my chin slightly, as I let the whale of sorrow drain back into my gut.

I've been studying

deep food lately: the chicken breast pulled from the bath of boiling oil to become a battered cloud in the sky's reflective window.

I asked Alyse to go out and take a picture of every piece of deep fried chicken she could find. But she didn't have a camera. So I went myself. Like Walker Evans, I figured.

The other deep food distortion is the American single—the marigold cheese slice protruding from under the bun and curling over the side of most burgers. The single is on the verge. It is about to melt, but still retains its angular physique. It is an allegory.

Did I tell you I have an actual Nazi flag that my Uncle Herbie brought back from Normandy. It was passed around the family until it landed in my closet next to a giant orange and black Baltimore Orioles flag that came from the old Memorial Stadium. I plan to sell it on eBay.

I was flying

back from LA when this somewhat bitchy flight attendant came down the aisle carrying a cute little basket of headphones. She was flagged down by an elderly woman in the seat across the aisle from me. The elderly woman was quite on the ball, for a woman in her late nineties. And she was traveling alone. I watched her dig through her purse with a shaky, sun-spotted hand. I studied her metacarpals, which I could see clearly through the saggy skin of her fingers. Her boney hand then emerged with two crumpled dollars.

But the flight attendant, bitch that she was, refused to accept the bills, asking for the elderly woman's credit card instead. The elderly woman didn't seem to understand the words *credit card*. Perhaps she had never used a credit card.

I had to act. I grabbed for my wallet, and waved my own credit card in the air, and said to the flight attendant, "Please put that woman's headphones on my credit card. OK?"

At this point the elderly woman thanked me, rose up from her seat, reached over, like, an entire row, and tried to stuff her dollars into my hand. I refused to take her money. But she kept trying.

The contemptuous JetBlue flight attendant swept my card indifferently, and handed me two headphones, one for me and one for the elderly woman.

"Did I ask for one?"

She looked at me with total confusion.

Hic

sunt leones was written on medieval maps. It meant: There are dragons ahead. Beware! You are now entering uncharted territory. Maybe you know this already.

When I searched for images corresponding with the phrase, I came across a dragon-lion etched by some Renaissance illustrator. The dragon-lion look exactly like Hoke!

Then I happened upon another picture of a very small dragon. This one was part dragon, part butterfly actually. It had sienna wings. And a flexible little ribcage. Its flame of breath appeared to be perfect for lighting cigarettes. I wanted to hold it in my hands. I wanted to glide my finger across its silky wings.

I wanted to blow into Hoke's nostrils and say all I have to say. And run my fingers through her black curly hair. And stick my fingers in the canals between her callused hairy pads that smell like Fritos brand corn chips.

144

I'm seated

next to this collector. And her Goldman Sachs fiancé. Then Eva walks over from the other table and I slide to the corner of my seat offering her the other corner. Across from us, sits the artist who has been painting a single glass of water for the last ninety years, or something.

Is the glass half empty or half full? Clearly it is both. Like the book I just read said, ambivalence is a spiritual matter. Indecision, on the other hand, is merely a character flaw.

I kid, darkly, that I plan to have one eye surgically replaced with a two-inch chrome steel ball. Leo attempted to translate my joke into German. Meaning without any humor. Leo and I both share one thing: nothing. No seriously, he's a cool guy. And I'm a cool guy. We share that. Is that conceited of me?

I introduce Eva as "my second wife." I thought it would be fine to refer to events that are unlikely to ever happen in the future (such as getting remarried to Eva) as if they've already happened in the past. Keep in mind, Eva and I are both still happily married to our own spouses.

Um, I was walking back to the subway when I stuck my hand into my coat pocket. What the hell? How did that get there? Earlier in the night, I must have set a plastic cup of wine, of all things, in my pocket, and forgotten about it. Who places a cup of wine in one's pocket? My fingertips were dripping.

I'm now Jeremy Reynolds. Did I tell you? A Brit. God, I'm awkward. I was introduced to a French woman and I totally screwed up the double kiss. I even ran into the guy that I stopped talking to five years ago. And I said, "I owe you an explanation." We agreed to sort it out at some point, which is when I plan to say: "In the future, don't criticize the Strokes."

Openings freak me out. I'm embarrassed for the art. I feel pure humiliation in the air. I sweat. Profusely. Like I do when I take my monthly lie detector test.

This afternoon I contacted someone online and asked him to please remove my picture. I said, "No offense, I'm simply trying to remove myself from the internet." I'd like to have no impact on the cyber environment. It's like cleaning up the camp site before the next hikers arrive.

The reporter

down on the street is like a lacrosse player at happy hour. His body language. His wrinkled oxford. As the city swarms. As kids pound on police cars. And stab fire hoses. Hundreds of looters giving fingers to helicopters. Teenage mothers spanking their teenage sons across their faces. A man ducks through the smashed out glass of a CVS and extends a 12-pack of Charmin to the heavens like a World Cup trophy.

The silver tadpole scares me with his lack of pigmentation. The way he latches on to Robert Valentine. Robert Valentine. You heard it first here. Well second. I'm no anchorman—nor am I an anchor poet. Nor is this news. But still. The vet says he's been through the "rice," and now possesses the courage to stand between shielded cops and taunting thugs…on the streets of Baltimore. As Gram Parsons once sang. Where is that song when we need it? Not that anyone ever needed it exactly.

My dad was interning at Hopkins in '68, when my mom, who was pregnant with me at the time, offered him an egg-beater bowl to wear on his head. She was worried that he'd get injured by rioters on his way downtown to put in a shift at the hospital.

I want to

make a mark. But with a new kind of marker. The kind with the delayed indelible ink. I'm working with a chemist to create an invisible ink that has a one-hundred year delay. This way in my lifetime, my poems will be invisible and unreadable, even to me. But will blossom once I am no longer here, and once I no longer consciously care. "Take my word for it," I say. "It will be poetry."

This guy actually claims to like my poetry. I keep saying "Prove it!" I don't trust that anyone has even *read* my poetry. At least not on a micro-tonal level. I don't trust that anyone has allowed it to actually beat down the door.

I'm also working with a wonderful MRI technician to measure a reader's brain while that reader is immersed in my writing. This way, I can edit the piece while looking at the affect it is having on different regions of the reader's brain.

If there is not an even mixture of pink and yellow and black and blue pixels in one specific region, it is then implied that I am a minor poet. At best.

I showered

With soap. With shampoo. With conditioner. My hair got fluffy. And frizzy. And fucking grayer. No whiter! I look like Bruce Dern in Nebraska. Older!

I emailed JA that I want his secretary to go over to him, pick him up off the Lay-Z-Boy, and give him a big tight bear hug for me.

I miss my gap. The gap I once had between my two front teeth. I wish I still had that meshugeneh grin across my face. My teeth, however, came together on their own. And the gap disappeared.

My brain, on the other hand, still hasn't come together. But I'm happy with myself. I'm bored of being the opposite. Now I just ask strangers flat out: "Am I too ugly for you to drop everything and kiss me?" And that kind of helps. I'm cheering up. Because I have an Emotional Support Dog. Her name is Chubby.

And my coffee plunger was recalled.

Cory said, "Tip says hi." That made me feel kind of on the map. Lena hasn't asked me to contribute any poems lately to her *Dead Horse Review*. I guess she's too busy being hilarious to care about poetry.

I'm writing this line for a muse from Kent who happens to get "funny." Like, the general idea of funny. Why do so many people miss my funniness?

I pretend to wake up on stage with an audience watching me pull on my socks. I belt out a Sondheim number in my apartment, as if I were facing the fourth wall. I project outward. Impel, as Charles Olson said. All the way to the back

148

row of the third balcony. I close the fourth wall when I need privacy.

Let's face it, none of us are on stage when we ought to be.

"It's alright to cry." From *Free To Be You and Me*. That's a damn good title for a book. I'd change it to: *Free to Be You, Fuck Me*. Or, *Free to Be Me, Fuck You*. Either. It's all the same. I want to stop writing now. But first I have to get this poem out of this rut.

I decided

to teach the film *Being There* as a play. Which required that I trade in my role as teacher for that of director. I was a brutal perfectionist. Trying to crack into my actors. Trying to scramble and unscramble their emotions. I almost broke a broomstick on one kid's face. After he failed to come through with the blood transfusion machine prop he promised he'd make. Then he dropped the class. Only to reappear in line for a ticket on opening night.

Vish had to learn to play Satie on piano. He enrolled at the nearby Peabody Conservatory. Essentially, he took a class at another college in order to pass my class. I guess you could say, I used another college and its professor to teach my class. Clever. And Ken learned *Basketball Jones*. A Cheech & Chong classic.

My Chauncey the Gardener was perfect. Lotfy. In a vintage executive bowler hat and a double-breasted pinstripe suit. It was the night of the dress rehearsal and we were running through the scene where Lotfy is supposed to pull down his pants in order for the doctor to give him a shot in the rear end. And he had on tighty-whities instead of boxers! I sort of lost it on him. "Why aren't you in character?! What part of dress rehearsal don't you understand?! And where are your sock garters?!"

I miscast my female lead. Even after Lauren warned me to focus on vocal projection. Rather than the curvature of her perfect ass.

It was amazing. Opening night. I had become this grizzly-bear-looking teacher, and I was tearing tickets at the door. Raking in 200 bucks. Which I promptly spent on pitchers that evening when I took the class full of minors out to the Tav.

Who knows what these

little structures imply. I make them as we talk. Some doodle. I set the crumbs into a microcosmic Stonehenge. Surrounded by commanding bottles of beer. Light is in no rush to run off. The room is still swirling in blush. Your eyes are just like mine. But wine. Bright, clear. More the opposite of mine. Mine feel heavy as felt. The white circular table is designed by Prouvé. I'll breathe and flex the floorboards, but first get cozy with the crew of pillows. Let out my belt. My salt and pepper combed into a bun.

The poet in Boston told me I was "chef-like," meaning: forgiven for being fat. When my life coach asked how she could help, I replied, "Tell me where to find a friend with benefits." But then I laughed, which proved, of course, that I was only kidding.

My lace

is undone. How? I just tied it. Double knotted it! I haven't gone anywhere. I'm right here at the bar. My bartender is married. She's a musician of what she calls Noir-something. She's my only Facebook friend. And I'm one of her three thousand, well, fans. Popularity is nothing to an individual. I sit down at the bar, grab a nice new cocktail napkin, borrow a pen and buckle down. My A.P.C.'s have a new crotch sewn in.

I was heartbroken by the documentary *Senna*. I've never seen such a face. Through such a windshield. Through his concentration I got it. Formula One! He drove to the death. His crash was always coming. Do I know this too? Do I feel this formula? My shoelace.

I just sat

down. Deep breath. The inner lining of my stomach has been chilly all day. Nerves. I brought in my jeans to A.P.C. It was a disaster. Another love of my life gone. I watched it tilt and plunge under the deep green sea. They were all looking at me funny. I must have looked as bad as I smelled. Sorry. Unwashed T-shirt. I showed him the exact spot where they were beginning to come unthreaded at the seam. "I would like a brand new pair," I said. And his reply made reference to the fact that they looked about 10 years old.

Bad behavior. But my poems need to behave badly. This is their way of confronting…well…something.

The best part of the reading was Hyde. Sitting third row center. Good posture. Bearded. Jolly. It was nice to see Eva too.

I went out to walk Hoke. Another cool summer night. Climate change has turned Brooklyn Heights into Maine. I dare not go on vacation. I won't even go to the Upper West Side. I was sitting on the stoop, when a girl I've seen around the hood stopped to pet Hoke. She asked me about Hoke's lion cut. I told her I was a writer. And she told me that she was a dog acupuncturist.

I want to

get away with something. You know? To cheat the system. Somehow. Really. Cheating is fun. I want to have an imperfect life. A body far too big for the shirts at J.Crew. I'm alive in Brooklyn. Still. Under a skylight. I'm nowhere close at all to anything.

Everyone working but me. In offices near and far. Cc-ing the entire population. Workers scattered around like rabbits in hard-helmets with hammers. Pig contractors in overalls up on scaffolding restoring the roof of the church across the street. Big sheets of copper.

There's a UPS drone hovering outside my window. It wants me to sign for my neighbor. Poets should look and act like Peter Falk. Don't you think? I could cheat the heat by wearing a wool sweater and hat indoors. Dieter taught me that. Is cheating the same as conserving? Cheating those who would otherwise capitalize off my cravings.

I cheated on the SATs. I failed to put my pencil down. They had to wrestle it out of my hand. That day I obnoxiously unlocked the emergency brake of Ben's Karmann Ghia and pushed it across campus so that he'd think it was stolen.

I had to cheat after I was electrocuted by my Telecaster. After my brain went limp. This is when my heart started pounding out a tablature of its own odd joy. While naked branches limbered up to meet the wind.

I'm just

a funny native who wants a little excitement. And laps in the pool give me time to play it through in my head. I feel like I've undergone some kind of interrogation. I'm a suspect. My crime: rhyme.

I have to stay confident. I have to stand naked in my boots. Like a man in a Larry Rivers painting. Like Eileen in her tie. But I can feel my mojo hemorrhaging. In a month it'll all be gone.

At the bar, I ran into the mothers. And I stopped to say hi. I made a joke that if I had gotten the Yale gig, I'd have started a secret other family up there in New Haven. Sorry. It was a Kahn reference. The mothers are deeply concerned about my unmarried-seeming ways. One of them commented that my Lacanian must not be helping me very much if I'm out at a bar this late on a Monday night by myself.

Finally. My book is out. Now I can go out in public. I gave Matvei a hug when I saw him at St. Marks. He rolled me a cig.

I had a great "Hi" with Pam, who smiled out of the crowd. My author copies fill a cardboard box. Here under my desk.

The voice inside my head is we. And we will see if we can write. The speakers will surround me like ten verbal morticians. A poem of voices will vibrate from a chorus of whispers. I guess it could be considered verbal treatment. I can't do it without you.

I no

longer look like someone in pain. Pain made me invisible. I now find myself in a nice conversation with the UPS woman. Or waving hello to Sammy the pet store owner. All the way across the street. Let's just say all the world is okay. For a day.

Fab wanted to know all the juicy details pertaining to my secretary. And I told her that it wasn't my job to tell stories. That I'm after something less cynical and more clinical. And that now is the time, if there ever was one, to drop anything that requires even a hint of ambition.

I watch

closely as my bartender rations off the last of the bottle into my glass. And I look out across the bar.

These kids want to put their lives on the internet because they want to monitor themselves. The mystery of who they may be is otherwise too great. They aren't able to let life lap up on their shores, one wave at a time. They have no feel for a change in the tide. For the shade that may come.

Or what may happen when they stay out of the spotlight. And stay in the moonlight. In the lovely lonely shadows? I say, "Break the rules before they break you."

The kids trade their cards of conformity. In the casino of ones and zeros. They sit thinking: I don't need to bluff. I have nothing to hide.

But you do! Don't you see? You do have to bluff. You do have something to hide. Play hide-and-seek with yourself.

And then this wild image comes to me. A culture that zigzags and shifts one way and back again. You know? I described it to Dan, as the Charlie Brown shirt. But more like a Barney Newman.

And a woman down the bar, turns her head towards me. Finally! I let my voice charge over the shoulder of my friend like a horse over a jump in a steeplechase. To that particular female person eavesdropping on my conversation. I got her to give it up. To crack a little smile. A tiny tinkle of appreciation. This talker needs to feel rewarded. I don't just sit here "tellin' it" for the benefit of a conversation. The eavesdropper. Now that's an audience. An audience of one. Pretending not to listen.

Do I have one in me?

Usually I can feel it. Right now I don't feel a damn thing. But wait! Look! My fingers are typing. Indenting keys. I feel like Glen Gould. At his first piano lesson. At like two. No. That seems old for Gould. He was already peaking at two. I guess I'm not gonna peak. And while I'm not entirely brain dead, I did blank earlier on my zip code, while trying to purchase Amtrak tickets on line. And the other day, I paused and tried to recollect if there was a dot between my first and last name.

Acknowledgements

The publisher and author would like to thank Erica Samuels for her generous support.

Further thanks goes to the author's family Cory Reynolds and Cole Sigler for their tolerance, support and unconditional love.

The author would also like to thank Alyse Ronayne who assisted in the early stages of some of the poems included in this book, as well as the editors and colleagues who published some of these texts in slightly different versions.

A SPOONBILL BOOK
Published by Spoonbill & Sugartown, Booksellers
218 Bedford Avenue
Brooklyn, NY 11249
www.spoonbillbooks.com

Distributed in the United States by
ARTBOOK | D.A.P.
www.artbook.com

Printed in Singapore by Pristone
First edition, 2017

ISBN: 978-0-692-76948-5

Cataloging-in-Publication data is available from
the Library of Congress.

Designed by Project Projects
Typeset in Monotype Garamond

Edited by Dan Nadel